The Book of the
A3 Pacifics

The daily scene that greeted the Shedmaster at King's Cross. Heaton's A3 60088 BOOK LAW is nearest, then the first Mikado, now rebuilt and a comparatively infrequent visitor from York, A2/2 No. 60501 COCK O' THE NORTH. The Cock looks as though he(?) has suffered a heavy shunt recently. The third engine is one of Grantham's 'Green Arrows', V2 No.60875, nicely clean and the fourth is A4 No. 60032 GANNET. The fifth is no doubt one of the home shed's fleet of A3s, unidentifiable sadly and the sixth is Thompson A2/1 Pacific No.60508 DUKE OF ROTHESAY, unmistakeably from New England in the normal livery of that depot. The details of the front of the engine are well displayed here, particularly the extended cover to the modified valve gear design. 1st November 1959. Alec Swain, The Transport Treasury.

A British Railways Illustrated Special
By
Peter J. Coster C.Eng, MICE, MCIT

Contents

First published in the United Kingdom in 2003
by Irwell Press Limited, 59A, High Street, Clophill,
Bedfordshire MK45 4BE
Printed by Newton Printing

THE A1 AND A3 PACIFICS OF SIR NIGEL GRESLEY

The story of the development of steam traction on the East Coast Route must be one of the best known and documented stories in steam locomotive history, if not the best. The rapid enlargement of steam locomotives under the leadership of Henry Ivatt was followed by the long tenure of Nigel Gresley, culminating in his magnificent Pacifics, Green Arrows and Mikados, and 126mph.

In this book we touch on the salient features of the story as they concern Gresley's first Pacifics of Class A1 moving on to his Class A3. The narrative and illustrations deal with the long history of these splendid locomotives, to which I have made my own comments as they seem appropriate. For many of us, these locomotives had a special place in our affections. Nigel Gresley built his Pacifics not just to look magnificent, but to work hard and efficiently. We start with his A1 Pacific No.1470, which was introduced in 1922, and move on to the A3, introduced in 1928. The work of these locomotives will be described and illustrated, up to the very last in service under British Railways. I have used the appropriate locomotive numbers for the period, and names, but I have used 24hr notation for times of day. I have also used the LNER classification rather than the GNR, to which it was very similar in principle, but different in detail.

I have written this short account of one of the most famous and well-loved steam locomotive designs as both a railway engineer and as a lifelong enthusiast. Although I have done many things in my professional career and in my leisure, I have not been fortunate enough to work with locomotives such as these. However it was my good fortune to know as friends many who did, and I have drawn much from what I learnt from them in this book. This account is written by an author who lived, as many did, at the south end of the East Coast main line, and therefore it is seen in that perspective. Although I have tried to cover events and situations overall, the stories and anecdotes lean towards the southern end of the line.

But why write about something that finished to all intents and purposes, a generation ago, and took place in two generations still farther back? Why indeed: the flames of controversy and the excitement of discovery and innovation have cooled long since. It no longer matters today. And the railway today is almost entirely different from that featuring in my narrative. Little remains – even the track is different. The story has been told before, many times, and probably in fuller detail.

We would be a poor nation if we did not also look back at the glory of earlier days in the last century, to when the world was much bigger in terms of travel, and to when our engineering was something of wonder and pride. When engineering was valued by the nation and its leaders and an engineer was more than someone with the technical skills to repair washing machines or fix a TV aerial. There are still many who remember the days of steam locomotives, of elegant coaches, of goods trains of all sorts, of service and safety. There are also preserved railways which allow us to see what a railway used to look like, and in which we can participate to discover how things were done half a century ago. Among our memories are the great locomotives which hauled our trains, and this book is a celebration of one of those designs, an exultation richly illustrated with photographs, most of which have not been used before.

I have set out to include an illustration of each engine at least once. I suppose any collection of photographs will include many of some but few of others. To all of us there were some often seen and photographed and some not, and their identities changed as one looks at different collections. Add to that particular inconsistency another, that of the photographer's measure of skill and the flair of some for having the wrong film, or setting, or camera at the vital moment, and one begins to understand how difficult illustration can be. Some engines are shown several times because the photographs are good, and in some cases getting one good illustration has been something of a battle.

The photographs used are from the Transport Treasury in many cases, and I am very grateful to Barry Hoper for the use of these wonderful photographs. My good friend John Aylard has contributed some of his superb work and the Revd Canon Brian Bailey, to whom the Revd A.C. Cawston's albums of railway photographs were bequeathed, has allowed me to use some of the master's work from his days at Grantham in the early 1930s. I hope you will agree that they all do Gresley's first Pacifics justice. To all photographers whose work is in these pages, whether used directly or indirectly, I would like to express my gratitude.

Admirers of the work of Sir Nigel Gresley will appreciate that not only did he build fine locomotives, but those locomotives always exhibited a fine quality in their appearance. His engines always had a beauty of line and proportion, a relatively timeless quality. The commemorative plaque at Edinburgh Waverley, installed with the kind permission of Railtrack, recalls this fact and illustrates it. Locomotive enthusiasts will always be in the debt of Alan Pegler, who bought BR No.60103 from British Railways. Not only did he do so, but it was despite the most antagonistic and mean-spirited behaviour by the BR Board which was hell-bent on eradicating all of "the old railway". Alan prevailed, preserved her as LNER No.4472 FLYING SCOTSMAN, and ran her, to the joy of enthusiasts especially those like myself for whom the LNER livery was a distant memory. And to the chagrin of her former owners, too. But for his initiative the entire class would have been withdrawn and cut up, and the world would never have been able to enjoy the sight and sound of one of the most handsome steam locomotives ever to be designed. She has subsequently passed through other hands, people who have all deserved our thanks, but thanks to Alan we can still see one of Sir Nigel Gresley's A3s in action in the country, arguably the most famous of all.

There is an enormous wealth of information about Gresley's A1 and A3 Pacifics, and much of the following story has been told before. There is a common fund of knowledge on all of our great locomotives, and I acknowledge that I have drawn freely upon this in writing the manuscript. There is much fine detail such as the nameplates and numberplates, the typeface used, the different boiler types carried at various times, left or right-hand drive, valve travel and maximum cut-off, and the minutiae of livery variations to fascinate the detectives among us.

Among these many reminiscences are those of friends were also engineers and enthusiasts who have passed on, but have left to later generations photographs, records and reminiscences to enrich our memories too. The illustrations are excellent, largely new (with, necessarily, a few 'old stagers' on the 'official' side) and I hope a considerable source of interest to those fascinated by what may be termed locomotive archaeology, and those who model railway locomotives.

I would like to thank in particular my friends George W. Carpenter C.Eng, M.I.Mech.E, Dr.Geoffrey Hughes and Peter N. Townend C.Eng, M.I.Mech.E, who have each contributed from their special knowledge and experience of Sir Nigel Gresley's first Pacifics. I am also greatly indebted for their help with the statistical information in the Appendices, to the compilers of the RCTS *Locomotives of the LNER* and to the late W.B. Yeadon's remarkable *Registers*. I should also include in my thanks M.B.Thomas, the former Public Relations & Publicity Officer of the old Eastern Region of British Railways at Liverpool Street for his patience with my many questions a long while ago. In addition, my thanks are due to my friends the Revd Canon Brian Bailey, Doug Landau, the Librarian of the NRM, C.P. Atkins, for assisting with the mileage information and Hugh Ramsey, for checking the manuscript

Finally I must thank my wife, Su, for her help and interest while I prepared this manuscript.

Peter J. Coster C.Eng, MICE, MCIT
Pendoggett Farm, St.Kew
Chairman, The Gresley Society Trust

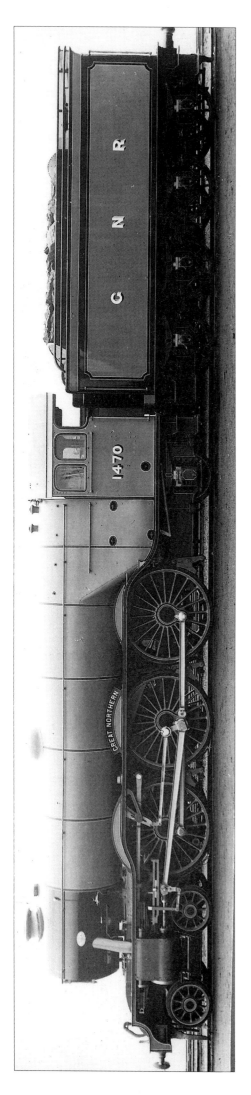

The official photograph of the original Gresley Pacific GNR No.1470 GREAT NORTHERN on release to traffic in April 1922. It was probably taken at Doncaster and, as was usual for official photographs, the background was removed. The engine has the prototypes of the Diagram 94 boiler (7646) and GNR style eight wheel tender (5211).

GREAT NORTHERN posing for a well-known photograph on the new turntable at King's Cross Station loco yard. By now the Doncaster engine is carrying its GNR number with an Area 'N' suffix as did a number of ex-GNR A1s. It is in the then new LNER livery of lined apple green. Early in the life of the LNER it was decided to transfer the engine number to the tender, and this was carried out at all workshops. A small numberplate was attached to the cab side in its place. The number dates the photograph as being taken between August 1923 and December 1924. The engine is still fitted with diagram 94 boiler (7646) and her GNR style eight wheel tender (5211).

CHAPTER ONE
PREAMBLE

As the railways of this country entered the 20th century, they were at the height of their commercial prowess. The Great Northern Railway was extremely successful and very competently managed. The Locomotive, Carriage & Wagon Department, under the leadership of their Superintendent, Henry Ivatt, had introduced larger and heavier coaching stock to cope with the demand. He had built his first Atlantic, No.990, in 1898, followed four years later by the first locomotive of the second series, class C1, the famous Ivatt Atlantics. This was a larger machine with a boiler increased from 4ft 8ins to 5ft 6ins in diameter. It was associated with a wide firebox for the first time, and as a result, the boiler was much higher pitched, making the locomotive look even more impressive. The greater power of the C1s was welcome, and the engines were strong and steamed well. They could be wild riders, a reputation that they never lost, even in their finest years.

In 1905, Ivatt's Superintendent in charge of Carriage and Wagon engineering, E.F. Howlden, retired and Herbert Nigel Gresley was appointed as his successor from Newton Heath Works on the Lancashire and Yorkshire Railway. At a time when age and experience counted for more than youth and energy, this was a remarkable appointment, for the post was senior and Gresley only 28 years old. In those days a career would be expected to peak in one's 60s, exceptionally perhaps in the mid to late fifties. H.N. Gresley was known his friends as Herbert, but he became publicly known by his second name, Nigel. A tall man, he was known to his intimates as (Tiny) Tim, but it was not a form of address he recognised outside the family.

The two worked happily until the autumn of 1911, when Henry Ivatt retired and Nigel Gresley, remarkably, was appointed in his place. The Directors of the Great Northern Railway, hitherto, had always appointed their Locomotive, Carriage and Wagon Superintendent from outside the Company, but here they made an appointment from within,

remarkable – indeed outstanding – for its insight and vision, for even now Gresley was only 35 years old. In passing they also made another far-reaching decision at about the same time in their Chief Civil Engineer, Charles H. Brown, who went on to serve with the LNER as Chief Engineer until 1936.

Henry Ivatt had been a fine leader and a good engineer, sometimes overlooked in the shadow of his illustrious successor. He had always believed that the most important function in a steam locomotive was its ability to boil water, and he had built a series of powerfully boilered locomotives for the Great Northern. In a seamless transition, Gresley took over, and his first locomotives continued the Great Northern style developed by his predecessor; indeed it seemed that the hand of Ivatt was apparent in the first Gresley engines. Gresley later became famous for his "Big Engine" approach to problems, but how much of that was due to the undoubted influence of Ivatt on Gresley

A3 No. 60108 GAY CRUSADER of King's Cross rests awhile in old platform 11 while the signalman sorts out a sudden rush with an incoming Leeds express into old platform eight and empty stock for departures. We thought nothing of her name, but it has acquired implications that were far from the mind in those days, as well as an historical irony. There was always a crowd at the end of platform 10 in steam days. Date summer 1957. Boiler 94A(27064) Tender GN(5266) Peter J. Coster.

The one that got away. Gateshead's No.60075 ST FRUSQUIN was overhauled in May 1961 and, by an administrative oversight, was not fitted with trough type deflectors. Here she stands at King's Cross, in old platform four in front of Walton's Fruit Store, with an overnight sleeping car express, just returned from Doncaster Works. Even the early morning commuter can't resist a moment to admire the A3. The different inspection holes of the diagram 107 boiler are particularly clear here. Boiler: 107 (29324, off A4 60028) Tender: GN 5257. Peter J. Coster.

in his earlier years we shall never know.

Gresley's ten years or so on the GNR were successful. He designed and built a mixture of heavy freight, what became known as "mixed traffic" types and tank engines such as the J50 and N2. The company was expanding its business with heavier and faster trains, and Gresley had not only to bear the burdens of the office in running what was in effect a major engineering enterprise, but to increase the power and performance of his fleet of locomotives. The first locomotive built during his period of office was actually Ivatt's Class J2 5ft 8ins 0-6-0 and it was not until 1912 when the first truly Gresley design appeared, No.1630, his handsome Class K1 2-6-0. Here Gresley demonstrated that he was quite willing to learn from others, and had noted the versatility of the Baldwin 2-6-0s of 1899 with their outside cylinders and valve gear, and the superior riding with a pony truck compared with the 0-6-0s and 0-8-0s of the GNR at that time. The K1s were developed into the K2 class with a 5ft 6ins boiler, a fine, rugged if rough riding engine that worked almost to the end of steam traction.

One of his major tasks was to improve the Ivatt Atlantics, the standard bearers of the Great Northern, which were felt to be capable of further development. Ivatt had built three experimental Atlantics, all compounds, in order to achieve greater power output, but without much success. Gresley rebuilt a fourth locomotive, No.279, as a four cylinder simple to assess the possibilities of four cylinders, but the experiment seemed not to achieve any great improvement either. Swindon, the acknowledged leaders in the field of locomotive development, had pioneered superheating in the UK and achieved an economy of 15% in coal consumption, but Churchward was doubtful about the effectiveness of lubrication at high temperature. Gresley experimented with various types of superheater, eventually settling for a 32 element Robinson type as the optimum solution.

The bulk of the class was rebuilt with piston valves and superheaters under the LNER, and the results were extraordinarily good from what was by then, compared with the Pacific, a medium sized express engine. This was due to the ability of the converted engines to produce superheated steam at very high temperatures of 800°F (approx. 430°C), increasing power output as a result. For decades they were a firm favourite on the southern end of the East Coast Route. Crews were prepared to put up with the minimal cab and sometimes wild riding so long as they would run and pull. Passenger traffic was growing rapidly, and it was not long before it had outgrown the large Atlantics. In the 1914-18 war heavy loads required the Atlantics to be piloted out of London to Potters Bar. Gresley had yet, however, to build a new express locomotive.

To the west, G.J. Churchward on the Great Western Railway was using four cylinders, inside valve gears and rocking shafts, congesting the space between the frames very much. He had subsequently considered three cylinders, but concluded that four cylinders with two sets of valve gear were preferable. In 1908 he built a Pacific, No.111 THE GREAT BEAR, but the Chief Engineer confined it to the London-Bristol route. The engine was large enough, certainly, but it was to all intents a "Star" with a much larger boiler and firegrate, and never substantiated its initial promise.

To the north Vincent Raven had used three cylinders on his Atlantics, but these were horizontal, in line abreast, driving the leading coupled axle and so required the use of relatively short connecting rods which increased angularity of piston thrust. On his 4-6-0s and Atlantics the connecting rods were also short and the inside mechanism was cramped, with three sets of Stephenson's link motion requiring six eccentrics on the leading crank axle. One wondered at the ability of the engines to run as well as they did but there was no doubt that the NER Atlantics and 4-6-0s were excellent machines.

It seemed that three cylinders were the simpler answer, but with the middle cylinder on the centreline, the valve gear had insufficient room for good access. There were the alternatives of divided drive as used successfully by Swindon, and compound drive which, though economically attractive, was more expensive to maintain and difficult to put into daily operation with its need for trained staff. Hence it was little favoured in Britain. The railway operating regime in France was very different, where the drivers were workshop trained and an understanding of compound drive could be relied upon. Not so in Britain, where at the time the driver was usually regarded as a self-trained artisan with little grasp of superheating and expansive working, let alone a three or four cylinder drive.

Gresley, having tried four cylinders on the Atlantics experimentally, opted for three. But how were they to be driven? He had decided upon concentrated drive, in other words having all three cylinders driving on to one crank axle. He had clearly rejected the Raven layout, and the consequence was a middle cylinder that had to be inclined for the connecting rod to clear the leading coupled axle. Conjugated valve gear to drive the middle valve spindle from the two outside had been pioneered by David Joy in 1886. Gresley patented his two versions in 1915. Whereas two sets of valve gear had been previously used in four cylinder simple or compound locomotives, enabling in the latter case control of the high and low pressure cylinders from a single reverser, Gresley's design sought to have the benefits of three cylinder drive without the encumbrance of a third inside valve gear. In May 1918 No.461, a three cylinder 2-8-0 prototype, appeared from Doncaster, the inside cylinder being driven by conjugated valve gear. In tests the three cylinder engine repeatedly demonstrated its superiority to No.456, a similar 2-8-0 locomotive but with two cylinders, in accelerating a heavy train on a gradient.

Design work had also been carried out on the GWR by H. Holcroft on a different version of the conjugated three cylinder layout. Although the system was not used by the GWR (since by then it was committed to four cylinder propulsion for its most powerful locomotives) it had been given serious consideration. Holcroft assisted Gresley with the piston valve layout for use with the latter's simplified horizontal conjugating mechanism. The result of his collaboration was the version that appeared on No.1000, the large Class K3 2-6-0 that appeared in March 1920.

Apart from experimental and Beyer-Garratt locomotives, the K3s were the first and the only British locomotives to carry parallel boilers as large as 6ft diameter which, with three cylinders and 5ft 8ins coupled wheels, made them powerful and versatile locomotives with a good turn of speed. In 1921 they handled 600 ton trains at average speeds of 50 mph during the coal strike, and in 1932 one was timed at 60 mph start-to-stop with 500 tons between Hitchin and Peterborough. Again, they worked right up until the end of steam. All of Gresley's engines without trailing axles provided considerable power within their length and, as a result, those without trailing axles were not good riders at best. When frames and axleboxes were worn, riding beggared polite description. The K3s were nicknamed "Jazzers" by their crews which, given their considerable capacity for speed, was hardly surprising.

So, by the early 1920s, the stage was set. The Government had decided to group the railways into "The Big Four" and the Great Northern Railway was due to join its neighbours as the London and North Eastern Railway.

No.60035 WINDSOR LAD standing at Haymarket. With this low level view it is possible to see the AWS receiver and protecting plate. The A3 has been fitted with a double chimney, but alas the old favourite was withdrawn early in 1961, and never had trough deflectors. Alongside is Carlisle Canal's B1 No.61217, an engine that went there new and remained there until withdrawn. In the background is Heaton's BOOK LAW. The date must be later than early 1959. Boiler: 94A (27001 or 58) Tender: Non corridor (5567) J. Robertson, The Transport Treasury.

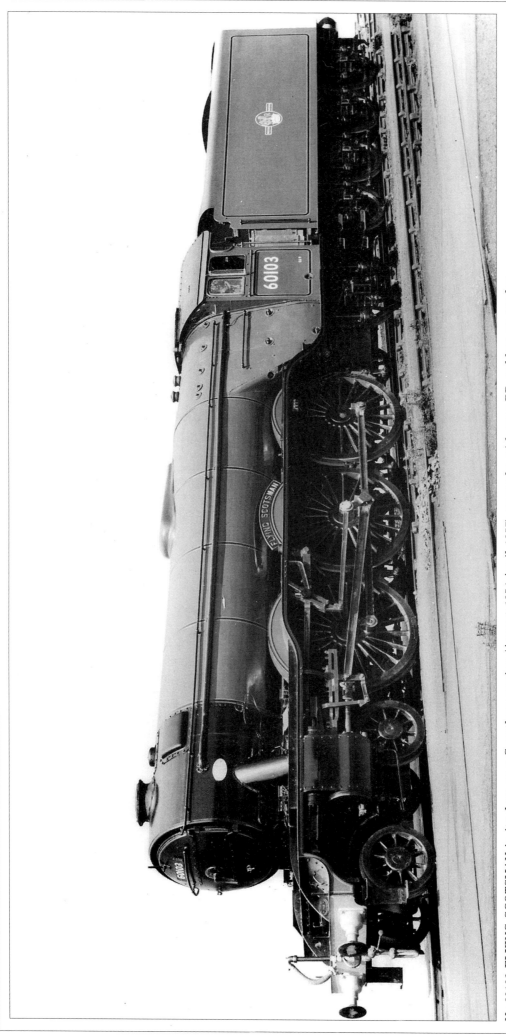

No.60103 FLYING SCOTSMAN in its days as a Grantham engine (August 1954-April 1957) ex-works with new BR emblem on tender.

CHAPTER TWO
A HISTORY

So now we come to the appearance in April 1922 of Gresley's first A1 Pacific, No.1470. It was one of the most sensational single advances in locomotive engineering that this country has seen. Of course there have been bigger and more powerful engines since, but Gresley's 1922 Pacific was a carefully calculated but nevertheless amazing leap forward into the future. That he succeeded so magnificently was due to his ability, his judgement, and his engineering instinct. It is the principal reason why he is rated as one of our finest locomotive engineers of all time.

The effect was astounding, for No.1470 was in size, apart from the GWR's solitary GREAT BEAR, by far the largest locomotive seen hitherto in this country. It must have been an extremely impressive locomotive to the railway world in 1922. Not only was it very large, but its appearance had a grace and balance which distinguished it as one of the most handsome engines ever to be built. No.1470 was named GREAT NORTHERN, a name carried above the middle splasher on a curved cast nameplate. Before very long it was joined by a second engine, No.1471, and an order was placed for a further ten engines. In September of the same year, No.1471 demonstrated that not only did she look powerful, but that she was just as awesome at work as she looked at rest. A test train of 610 tons

was worked to Grantham and back with comparative ease. Later No.1471 was named SIR FREDERICK BANBURY after the last Chairman of the GNR.

The appearance and particularly the choice of boiler for No.1470 puzzled some of the observers of the day. As well they might, for nothing in the development work hitherto had suggested that this was the direction which Gresley was taking. The experimental work preceding the design of the A1 seemed to contribute nothing to the final design. In fact it was useful in evaluating and eliminating ideas which would have restricted both the design and its development had they been used. One basic influence was the superheated K4s Pacific of the Pennsylvania Railroad, which used a large boiler formed of a leading parallel section mated to a rear conically tapered section. Whereas the K4s had a wide Belpaire firebox however, Gresley opted for a round-top firebox with a wide grate, a simpler and cheaper arrangement. Once the boiler design had been fixed, it was a simple matter to adapt the K3 front end layout to the larger engine. In this latter respect it differed essentially from the Pennsylvania machine.

The frames of the Ivatt Atlantics were extended back under the cab and a carrying axle was provided, rather

than a separate Bissel truck or similar design. While there was lateral tolerance, there was no control on lateral movement, which no doubt contributed to the engine's lively riding. No.1470 was a far longer and larger locomotive and, clearly, to provide the necessary flexibility in the locomotive wheelbase to negotiate sharply curved connections in depots and station yards, something more was required. Gresley's solution was to use Cortazzi axleboxes (normally erroneously called 'Cartazzi') which allowed lateral movement, but the weight of the locomotive acting on inclined sliding top faces of the axleboxes gave a self-centring control. The arrangement served for four decades trouble-free on all the designs that followed.

The provision of a large cab with a good lookout was copied from the Great Eastern Railway's "Claud Hamilton" 4-4-0, built at the turn of the century, and as such was ahead of its time. Unusually, drivers had a steam chest pressure gauge as well as a boiler pressure gauge. Cabs had improved in twenty years on the GNR since the introduction of the Ivatt Atlantic. Drivers and firemen had padded seats, modified in 1935 to the "bucket" seats used in the A4s and V2s, and a 1929 addition was the small cabside glass which deflected the slipstream away from the driver's face as he looked ahead.

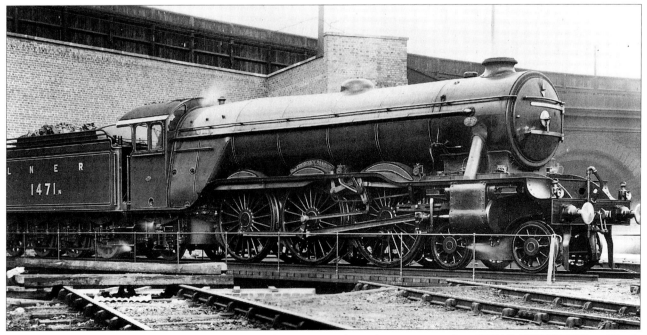

No.1471N SIR FREDERICK BANBURY, in a similar pose to sister Doncaster engine GREAT NORTHERN at King's Cross Station loco yard, having just reversed on to the new turntable. The A1 is also in LNER livery and her GNR number has the LNER Area suffix on the tender side, and the small cabside numberplate. The date probably lies between August and December 1923, but the LNER number may not have been applied at the first overhaul, in which case the date may be later. The name was that of the Chairman of the GNR. Such names were never a happy choice, but it ensured that the name was remembered long after the bearer had been forgotten. Boiler: 94 (7647) Tender: GN (5212). Courtesy G. Goslin, The Gresley Society.

The first A1s were too long to be turned in London, and had to run four miles out to Hornsey and back tender first. GREAT NORTHERN, in GNR livery and bearing a GNR number is at Hornsey in early 1923. The GNR livery was apple green with slightly more ornate black and white lining, applied in panels on the cab and tender, and the edging outside the panels was in a darker olive green. Boiler: 94 (7646) Tender: GN (5211).

The regulator was a pull-out type, widely used in North America, which in wartime and post-war maintenance conditions could sometimes become appallingly stiff. The reverser was a vertical screw column type, which again could become difficult to move when stiff. It was sometimes necessary for the driver to move out of the driving seat and stand facing the reverser in order to adjust it, to avoid strain. When properly maintained, adjusted and greased, as one can see on the preserved locomotives, these conveniently located controls are easy to use. All too often, when engines were run-down, they were not. These two features could be responsible for some spectacularly volcanic starts when the engine concerned was run down – and the East Coast main line had few stations that provided an easy start for a Pacific. The engines were coupled to large rigid frame eight wheel tenders with coal rails of typical GN outline.

There followed twelve A1s ordered by the GNR but built mainly by the London and North Eastern Railway, which came into being on January 1st 1923. The last of the twelve GNR engines, ST SIMON, was completed to the North British loading gauge, which was less generous. It was loaned to

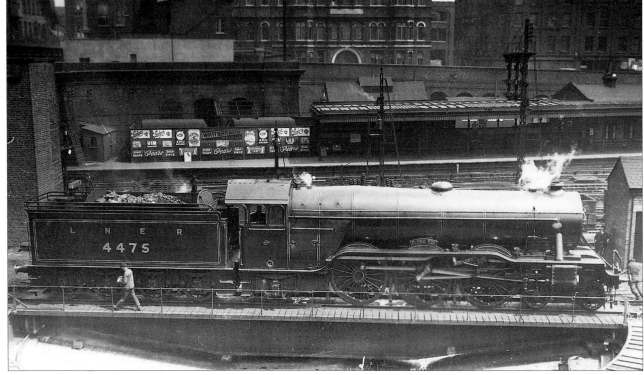

The second King's Cross A1, FLYING FOX, stands on the turntable at the station. The A1 has acquired its correct LNER number, carried on the tender. The date is between February 1925 and July 1928 when long travel valves were fitted. Boiler: 94 (7696) Tender: GN (5226). An interesting feature of this shot is the foot treads round the turntable, which were necessary before the provision of a vacuum engine powered from the locomotive's main ejector to (help) turn the engine. Manual turntables were known colloquially as Armstrong turntables, for obvious reasons. Courtesy G. Goslin, The Gresley Society.

The first King's Cross A1 was the grand old favourite VICTOR WILD, although it was simply LNER No.4474 in 1925. Driver Pibworth is seen here bringing his A1 through Westbury on the "Cornish Riviera Express", a good load, 14 on. Compared to the normal "Castle", the A1 must seemed enormous. Boiler: 94 (7695) Tender: GN (5225).

Gateshead shed for six months at the end of 1923 and, as Willie Yeadon says in his *Register*, it argued with the copings on the sharply curved platforms at Newcastle Central while on test. Gateshead Works removed the front footsteps and notched the buffer beam and eventually these changes spread to the entire class. The NB loading gauge did, however, allow the provision of a high cab ventilator, which lasted many years, first on ST. SIMON and then on MERRY HAMPTON after its derailment in 1947.

The North Eastern Railway, keen to maintain its dominant position in the new company, rushed out a Pacific design, No.2400, very late in 1922. Like No.1470, it had a large boiler with a large firegrate and combustion chamber, and an even longer smokebox, but its driving mechanism was clearly a stretched version of the Raven Atlantic. Whereas the latter was a fine engine, the Pacific was not so much of an improvement as its size suggested, its cramped inside layout leaving little scope for easy maintenance. It was a clear endorsement of Gresley's wisdom in setting his face against merely enlarging Ivatt's Atlantic. Before the new company placed orders for new engines, the Pacifics of Gresley and Raven were tested between London and Doncaster. Although the Gresley A1 prevailed, the results were much closer than people expected. Indeed, judged on performance alone, the NE Pacific was driven harder and ran well, largely due to the efforts of Driver Tom Blades and Fireman Charlie Fisher, one of

Gateshead's most senior crews. When the fuel consumption was compared, it was the A1 which was the more economical and it was this, coupled with design features which Gresley was not prepared to perpetuate, which justified the choice of the A1 for future building. There is no doubt that the NE Pacific had shown up much better than was generally expected largely due to the skill and enthusiasm of her crew.

So another forty A1s were ordered by the LNER, twenty from Doncaster and twenty from the North British Locomotive Works at Glasgow. The Doncaster engines went to former GN depots, now the LNER Southern Area. Of the NBL engines, five went to Scotland and fifteen were fitted with the Westinghouse compressed air brake, going to the NE Area at Gateshead and Heaton sheds. They were also fitted with the Raven fog signalling apparatus that was in use at the time, but when the experiment was discontinued, the equipment was removed. At Grouping the North British Railway was in a poor state, and an infusion of motive power from the south was necessary. The condition of the NBR track was also poor, and the Pacifics were intended principally for the East Coast main line to Edinburgh. Haymarket shed at Edinburgh had, until then, fulfilled only a minor role in the working of the East Coast main line.

The third engine, No.1472, was renumbered 4472 and exhibited in the Wembley exhibition of 1924 alongside the first of the Great Western Castle

class, No.4073 CAERPHILLY CASTLE. The A1 was named FLYING SCOTSMAN, immaculately prepared to an exhibition finish and looked superb. Due to space limitations it was exhibited with a K3 tender. Whereas the A1 boiler was pitched with its central axis level, the GWR pitched its taper boilers with the bottom of the boiler level, making the locomotive appear smaller than was the case when viewed from the front. This was always a problem for photographers of GWR engines, trying to convey a sense of their undoubted power and speed, especially low down at the trackside.

So visitors to the exhibition were surprised to see that the GWR claimed that their engine was "the most powerful express engine in Great Britain". This was on the basis of calculated maximum tractive effort at starting, a concept that did not take into account the steam producing capacity of the boiler. The Castle was a very good 4-6-0, and the secret of the design was the long lap and long travel valves, which when coupled with the excellence of the other design features, made it both very effective and efficient. The A1 initially had shorter valve lap and travel: longer travel had been tried with the K3s, but trouble had arisen with the valves overrunning at speed, and Gresley had reduced the valve travel temporarily while the cross bracket supporting the main 2:1 beam of the conjugated gear was redesigned for greater rigidity.

However, a challenge had emerged from General Manager circles – something, it appears, that Gresley

VICTOR WILD at speed with the "Cornish Riviera Express" on the Exchanges. The location is not stated, but I would plump for somewhere between Westbury and Castle Cary. The A1 was a right-hand drive engine, and the empty cab has a slightly unnerving appearance. Boiler: 94 (7695) Tender: GN (5225).

knew little about. Work was proceeding at Doncaster on the conjugated valve gear and although he subsequently needed a deal of pressure to act, he must have felt some doubts about a very public trial of strength and economy. Nevertheless, in April 1925, No.4474 of King's Cross was sent to run for two weeks on the GWR to work the Cornish Riviera Express to Plymouth and back. It should be explained that the A1s ran for a period after building before the nameplates were added. The nominated engine was in fact No.4475, which ran hot. There were considerable difficulties – with the unfamiliar Welsh coal, with learning an unfamiliar road with much reverse curvature and with running such a large locomotive at speed on a winding route with no transition curves to speak of. The GWR track was good for its day, but No.4474 was a severe test. The GWR's own Pacific, THE GREAT BEAR, as referred to already, was banned from the Plymouth road due to its greater axle load than the Star class.

One can understand Driver Alf Pibworth's reluctance to run fast on a strange road, and the need to repair various pipe joints around the locomotive between turns showed that he was wise not to try running faster. Also, even with a helpful conductor, it was difficult to prepare the firebed sufficiently far ahead for frequent changes of gradient on a strange road. That said, No.4474 steadily improved her running and achieved some highly creditable uphill performances. Her opponent, No.4074 CALDICOT

CASTLE, driven hard by Driver Edward Rowe, had a clear road and ran superbly. It might be thought strange that one could run fifteen minutes early and not be checked, but whether the GWR management did a little stage managing or not it was magnificent running. There was no doubt which was the more economical machine, although the final runs by No.4474 were much improved and the differences became very small. The uphill speeds of No.4474 were in fact better than the best efforts of No.4074 and as the A1 crew and their locomotive acclimatised on the GWR, they were beginning to give the crew of the Castle a run for their money!

On the LNER, hopes that the story would be different were misplaced. No.4475 ran hot again, and her replacement, No.2545, had trouble with her sanding gear, and ran poorly. Driver Ben Glasgow was, by all accounts, not the most skilled member of the top link, but in fairness his formative years had been spent on saturated 4-4-0s and 4-4-2s. In those days one had to learn from one's seniors, for there was no official training, and he like many others tended to use long cut-offs and a partially open regulator, which gave a calmer ride but to the detriment of his coal consumption on the Pacifics. It had been the normal practice to drive on the regulator, probably due to the difficulty in notching up the Atlantics, with their lever reverser. Unfortunately Gresley had lost control of footplate staff with the formation of the LNER. Whilst he had advised enginemen on

how best to handle his engines, no sign of that survived long into the LNER.

The Castle was No.4079 PENDENNIS CASTLE, and although Driver Young gained time, it was the ability of No.4079 to start a very heavy train without the slightest trace of a slip that impressed. This was particularly noticeable from Kings Cross up the 1 in 105 to Holloway and the 1 in 200 from Alexandra Palace (Wood Green) to Potters Bar. The East Coast main line had many difficult starts due to gradient and curvature but Driver Young took No.4079 away cleanly every time. What was also noticeable was that coal consumption was relatively high, albeit lower than No.2545, and Fireman Pearce no doubt had more trouble with Yorkshire coal than was at first admitted. The LNER had certainly not had much luck with their engines, but the GWR engine was undoubtedly the better performer of the two on LNER metals.

The GWR had a well developed publicity expertise, and made the most of their engine's exploits. This caused some bitterness at the time since it was not intended to divulge details of the tests for publicity purposes. As the leading commentator on locomotive performance, Cecil J. Allen, was a member of the LNER staff and had given his view on the Exchange, the GWR felt not unreasonably that the matter was now in the public domain. The "weighed-on and off" system of comparing locomotive performance has its limitations, and all testing of locomotives is subject to mechanical failure, variations in coal and firing, bad weather and many other manifestations of Murphy's famous behavioural observations. Technical opinion regarded the trials as too short and inadequately prepared, as there were many issues unaddressed. Performance had not been related to drawbar horsepower, for example. Nevertheless, the GWR held that its claim to greater power had been substantiated, and Gresley was left to ponder on the results. His report to the Board is in the *Appendices*.

In the previous year Gresley's Technical Assistant Bert Spencer had put forward the case for redesigning the Pacific valve gear with longer valve travel and lap, and only a month before the Exchanges the subject had been discussed again. It was felt to be too costly for an immediate modification on 52 new locomotives, and the LNER was not a wealthy company. In 1925, the GWR was quite secretive about technical matters, but in that year three Castles appeared on LNER metals. No.4079 was working between King's Cross and Doncaster, and Nos.111 (formerly THE GREAT BEAR but by then rebuilt as a 4-6-0 and named VISCOUNT CHURCHILL) and 4082 WINDSOR CASTLE were at Shildon for the Stockton and Darlington Centenary celebrations.

At least one set of Castle valve gear was measured carefully in strict secrecy at an advantageous time in the absence of the crew, as a control check on Spencer's proposed design. Accounts of the incident vary, involving 4079 at Doncaster or 4082 at Darlington, or both. Whether the valves were dismantled and measured, or simply measured, is unclear, but senior men have acknowledged that such an event did indeed take place. If the engine's tender handbrake was screwed down hard and the coupled wheels scotched so that the engine did not move, the outside valves, being driven by rocking levers, could be uncoupled, dismantled, measured and reassembled in a few hours without the valve events being disturbed. It was, however, quite possible to establish the salient dimensions without dismantling anything at all. It is hard to believe that if it was done, it had Gresley's authority. As mentioned already, under Collett the GWR was careful about what information was divulged, and after one encounter with the GWR's publicity machine over the Exchanges, perhaps the LNER was reluctant to seek details of GWR valve gear publicly.

The dimensions were found to be very similar to Spencer's design. After the Castle had been measured, the results were transferred to the valve gear model at Darlington. Soon after, the valve gear of No.4477 was modified cheaply on an experimental basis, but the improvement was not considered to be worth the cost. Gresley still felt that the improvement was not

worthwhile as the existing gear was performing satisfactorily. However, Spencer had regarded the 4477 experiment as inadequate, and persisted in seeking a proper trial of the fully redesigned gear. Authority had been given in early 1926 to change the piston valve rings from a single broad ring to four narrow rings, which had an important effect in reducing wear and steam leakage and hence coal consumption. In late 1926 Gresley yielded, and new valve gear with the new rings and the longer valve travel and lap on the first conversion, No.2555 CENTENARY had a dramatic effect. In comparison with the unmodified A1, No.2559 THE TETRARCH, the reduction in coal consumption was over 20% and the water consumption even more. Driven with full regulator and a short cut-off, the modified A1 was now a powerful and economical locomotive.

Gresley, returning from Doncaster, found CENTENARY at the head of his train and made the journey on the footplate of No.2555 to see its performance for himself. Having observed how economically she ran, he authorised the conversion of all A1s straightaway. One might think that a change from 4.5625 to 5.75ins in valve travel and 1.25 to 1.625 in steam lap (at full cut-off) is insignificant, but it made a considerable difference to the working of the engines. The redesigned valve gear would not fit under the existing running plate, necessitating the widening of a casing that originally formed part of the smokebox saddle. It enabled the same power to be developed at full regulator with 25% cut-off on the modified locomotives as at 40% with the original A1s. There is evidence, however, to suggest that the short valve travel A1s could be handled more economically, in the right hands. The handicap of lower power outputs at short cut-offs remained, caused by the lesser steam flow and lower expansion through the smaller valve apertures. Too many of the older men though, like Driver Ben Glasgow, were not receptive to new ideas.

Gresley had taken the view that the higher boiler pressure of the Castle had saved a little coal, but that saving was offset by the additional boiler maintenance and increased scale formation. However, he seems to have decided to investigate the whole question for himself, together with that of compounding associated with high boiler pressure. The Chief Civil Engineer had authorised an increase in axle loading from 20 to 22 tons, so Gresley ordered five new boilers with thicker plates to work at 220 psi early in 1927. This was to ascertain for himself their effect on costs, but also with a view to providing a greater reserve of power for heavy loads and steep gradients. Gresley had been dissatisfied with the degree of

superheat being achieved in the A1 boilers and so in 1925 had had two boilers built, Nos.7779 and 7781, equipped with the Superheater Co's type "E" double superheater elements which were used on A1 No.2562 ISINGLASS and P1 Mikado No.2393. The effect was almost a reversal of proportions between the heating surfaces of the tubes and superheater, resulting in an enormous increase in superheat. In practice this did not significantly raise the steam temperature achieved and on test against No.2570 TRANQUIL the steaming appeared to be less satisfactory. The extra superheating surface was not so effective as the Robinson elements normally used on the A1 boilers. The new diagram 94HP boilers were equipped with much larger 43 element superheaters, and while Gresley was always prepared to accept any modification considered worthwhile, the 94HP and 94A boilers served him well. Several different types of superheater element were tried later using a different shape, such as the Sinuflo. Each of these types sought to lengthen the path through which passing steam was exposed to higher temperatures without retarding the flow, but no significant improvement was found.

North Eastern Area A1s had stalled twice on the 1 in 96 of Cockburnspath and had needed the services of a banker to get moving again. On one occasion the load was as little as 351 tons. Tests between Newcastle and Edinburgh had been carried out in 1925 and it was clear that, for very heavy loads, the Pacifics needed even more starting power. No doubt this was in Gresley's mind, for three of the new boilers went to NE Area Pacifics. Quite separately, he decided to build a high pressure compound 4-6-4, No.10000, and Darlington started work on the design. It had been decided, however, to use a Yarrow marine type water tube boiler pressed to 450 psi and so few lessons learnt with the compound could be applied to conventional locomotive boilers.

The first two new boilers were fitted to No.4480 ENTERPRISE in July 1927 and No.2544 LEMBERG in December 1927, the first with the A1 cylinder size unaltered and the second with lined-down 18¼in cylinders to give an approximation of the A1 tractive effort. The tractive effort of No.4480 was increased by 22% as a result, and she was reclassified A3, the first of the class. The designation was subdivided for a period, A3/1 referring to No.4480, A3/2 to No.2544 and the new engines from No.2743 onwards forming Class A3/3. In February 1928 No.2544 was tested against No.4473 SOLARIO, a 180 psi engine but, curiously, No.4480 was omitted. The massive increase in tractive effort had made No.4480 more prone to slipping, and it required

The rivals. The second part of the 1925 Exchanges was on the East Coast main line, and the two contestants were posed at King's Cross Top Shed. The photograph was a time exposure as the background indicates, and the orthochromatic emulsion of the plate made the apple green livery of FLYING FOX appear very much lighter. The darker GWR green of PENDENNIS CASTLE had more red in its composition and is more accurately portrayed. In the event FLYING FOX unfortunately ran hot and DIAMOND JUBILEE was substituted. Boiler: 94 (7696) Tender: GN (5226).

careful handling. The tests were well monitored, and the conclusion was that there was little in it. With two locomotives in which the differences were relatively small, that was hardly surprising. It was noticeable however, that No.2544 was a faster engine, and the slight advantage she possessed in water consumption could be due to full regulator operation with short cut-offs, and the freer steam flow resulting from the better balance between 8in piston valves and 18¼in cylinders as much as higher boiler pressure.

The three other boilers went to Darlington as mentioned above, where they were used on Gateshead's No.2573 HARVESTER and Heaton's Nos.2578 BAYARDO and 2580 SHOTOVER, all initially retaining 20in cylinders. Later the A3 cylinder diameter was standardised at 19ins. With 20in cylinders, running at 15% cut-off the power developed was such that, with existing schedules, the regulator was partially closed, reducing efficiency. A test run had been made in March 1927 with A1 No.2563 WILLIAM WHITELAW hauling 400 tons over the severely graded Waverley route from Edinburgh to Carlisle. This had been the first time a Pacific had worked over the line. Much of it was restricted to moderate speeds and, bearing the severe gradients and curvature in mind, and the fact that much of it was only ash ballasted, I would imagine a special dispensation would have been required from the Chief Civil Engineer. The driver, not having had a trial run first, was unfamiliar with both engine and road

and was therefore over-cautious; to make things worse, poor coal was taken on at Carlisle Canal shed. The important conclusion was that the A1 needed greater power for this sort of load and route. The tests were repeated a year later, this time with the 220 psi No.2580 hauling 400 tons, with far more success.

In August 1927, hardly more than a month after ordering the five 220 psi boilers, ten new engines of Class A3 were ordered. As Gresley had previously been doubtful about the wisdom of going for higher pressure this seems odd, but in providing a larger control group the final decision could be made on a broader basis. One suspects that Gresley was gradually accepting the need for higher pressures, also encouraged by the improved water treatment directed by his new Chief Chemist, T. Henry Turner.

Meanwhile, the improvement in Pacific efficiency generally had enabled the operators to work them over longer distances, from London to Doncaster as a previous maximum, on to York and then Newcastle. Their economical performance had encouraged the LNER to run the "Flying Scotsman's" relief non-stop from London to Newcastle, 268 miles, in 1927. The train concerned was the 9.50 TWX and the 9.30 from Newcastle; through running started on July 11th of that year with Driver Pibworth on FLYING FOX and Driver Blades on GLADIATEUR. Competition with the LMSR had started to flourish, and the LMSR had made much of its London-Carlisle

running (299 miles) in winter 1927. The LNER replied in 1928 with *daily* non-stop running between London and Edinburgh on the "Flying Scotsman" service, always known as the "Non-stop" to railwaymen.

This was a considerable increase, all but 125 miles, over what had only just been achieved the year before. The coal capacity for the A1s and A3s with long valve travel was comfortably adequate, but the relatively close spacing of water troughs on the GNR was not replicated on the NER section. There were none on the North British Railway beyond Berwick. Water usage therefore had to be managed quite carefully over the northern half, with 98 miles between the two NE sets of troughs at Wiske Moor and Lucker. The more expert drivers habitually ran the 124.5 miles from Newcastle to Edinburgh without taking water at Lucker. No.2582 SIR HUGO worked a trial run from York to Edinburgh with 350 tons in January 1928 and the average lift of water was just below 2,000 gallons. This was too little, and after improving water delivery to the troughs at each site, another run was made on February 10th with No.2568 SCEPTRE now hauling 450 tons, and nearly 2,500 gallons were lifted.

One other problem remained: to accomplish this task, two crews were needed for the distance, without question. A means of crew changing without stopping was required. This was the reason for the construction of the famous corridor tenders, the largest to run in Britain and a brilliant solution. Ten of these relatively huge

No.2554 WOOLWINDER, another Doncaster engine, climbing to Stoke from Grantham, in the deep cutting between Great Ponton and Highdyke. The A1 has a good load behind, probably from Leeds and Bradford. She is in original condition with short travel valve gear, which places the date between 1925 and early 1930, but I would surmise that the number would have moved to the cab side after the 1929 overhaul, if not the 1928. Boiler: 94 (7772) Tender: GN (5264) Michael Mensing Collection.

No.2550 BLINK BONNY in King's Cross station, by the loco yard. The A1 has been fitted with long travel valves and is working from Grantham. Doncaster Works reverted to cabside numbers with the building of the corridor tenders since these had an independent existence, moving from locomotive to locomotive as necessary. At least one record exists of a locomotive changing its tender hurriedly and thus becoming anonymous. It happened on May 3rd 1928, when a corridor tender was hastily attached to DONOVAN in order to replace FLYING SCOTSMAN on the "Non-stop", with the result that neither engine nor tender had a running number on the cab side or tender. (Of course there was one on the front buffer beam for those who were close enough). It was decided to move the number back to the cab side and the tender simply carried the initials of the company. The new A3s were liveried accordingly and the A1s were altered similarly. The valve conversion, cabside glass screens and the numbering put the date at 1929-30. Boiler: 94 (7696) Tender: GN (5260).

tenders were built in a short time. The first were fitted to the first three A3s, but then were coupled to A1 and A3 locomotives selected for the "Non-stop", and the displaced GN tenders used with the new engines.

The "Non-stop", as it was known in railway circles, was more a matter of easy working and economy at first. It was claimed that only the long valve travel A1s could work the service: certainly only they could work it comfortably within coal capacity. The original engines would, if handled carefully, have probably coped, but with a much greater risk of running out of fuel. The Railway Races of 1895 had resulted in a commercial agreement between the parties of the East and West Coast routes not to compete, and this remained in force with an 8¼hr schedule. In 1932 the LNER and LMSR agreed that this should come to an end. The schedules were relatively lengthy due to the agreement, but with its cessation, they came down to a 7½hr timing from London to Edinburgh. With a heavy train, this was a harder proposition. It was later reduced to 7¼ hrs and in 1938 to 7hrs.

Over the years, several have questioned the viability of this service as it only ran for the summer months, and it was eventually dropped with the disappearance of steam traction.

Overall it would have been minimal in its effect on revenue one way or another. With departure of steam traction crews could not easily be changed on diesel traction without stopping, and nearly 400 miles in either end of a "Deltic", with the noise levels prevailing, was unacceptable. Steam haulage finished in 1961, and for the 1962 season experimental prototype diesel-electric DP2 dominated the running, albeit with a stop at Newcastle. That was the last season. It is difficult in the 21st century to judge the effect that this change made to the LNER and its fortunes, but it was corn in Egypt to the nascent publicity section. It was popular with the public, whose journey was undisturbed by intermediate stops, and its record of service was unblemished. I remember the "Non-stop" from the late 1940s and 1950s, and as the showpiece of LNER operating, locomotive and rolling stock departments – later the E, NE and Scottish Regions of British Railways – it was without equal. It encouraged team spirit and generated both motivation and publicity.

So in August 1928 the first of the new A3s came out of Doncaster, No.2743 FELSTEAD, followed by another nine, Nos.2744-2752. Another batch of eight came out in 1930, Nos.2595-2597, 2795-2797, and 2598-

2599, and the final batch of nine came out in 1934/35, Nos.2500-2508, 27 engines in all. The final batch of five was increased to nine to allow for the withdrawal of the Raven Pacifics. The tenders of the A3s at first were either corridor ones or the GN type that the corridor tenders had displaced. Commencing with No.2595 of the 1930 build, a new high sided tender, No.5476, appeared, based on the corridor tender design. An eleventh corridor tender had been built afterwards at Doncaster for the "Hush-hush" high pressure compound No.10000, being built at Darlington. Once all the GN tenders had been re-coupled to new A3s, tenders of the new type were built for further engines. The corridor tenders were moved around independently, coupled to engines as traffic required. One of the 1928 batch, No.2744 GRAND PARADE, was damaged beyond economic repair in the 1938 Castlecary collision near Glasgow, and a 28th new engine was built as a replacement. In fact, the new engine was substantially complete by the time the original had been made roadworthy and towed to Doncaster.

The A3s were magnificent engines, and they were referred to as "Super-Pacifics" in the 1930s. They were marginally more powerful than the A1s, on the steeper grades especially so. As a result of both this and a natural wish to standardise, it was decided not to build any more 180 psi diagram 94 boilers. A small economy in favour of the 220 psi boiler engines had been achieved, so when an A1 boiler was no longer serviceable and the spare boilers had been used, the engine was rebuilt to Class A3 and fitted with a 220 psi 94HP or 94A boiler. The first conversion was in November 1939, No.2566 LADAS of Haymarket, followed by a general conversion from 1941 onwards as the old boilers wore out, although the process was lengthy due to the longevity of the 180 psi boilers.

The last batch of A3s, Nos.2500-2508, were equipped with a banjo-shaped steam collector in place of a dome, and larger 7 ins main steam delivery pipes. As early as 1924 the Superheater Co. had advised Gresley that the main steam delivery pipe should be enlarged from 5 ins. The banjo dome reduced the carry-over of water droplets in the steam. This was the diagram 94A boiler. The superheater elements were of the sine wave type that had been tested by Doncaster, and used on the first P2 Mikados. No significant improvement was achieved and normal Robinson elements took their place. Of course, when an engine went to Doncaster for general overhaul and the boiler needed repair, it was lifted and removed to the Boiler Shop. When the engine was re-erected the next suitable repaired boiler available was fitted, and any connection between the engine and its previous boiler was lost.

The frames of the A1s had given some trouble with cracking, due to the use of lightening holes to reduce weight, and a progressive frame redesign to provide greater strength was carried out. The use of the middle driving axle for the drive from all three cylinders meant that it was difficult to brace the frames adequately around the driving axle, and the forward end had to leave space for the middle connecting rod to operate. The A3 frames had no cut-out sections and were stronger and more reliable as a result, although frame cracking still occurred. Faced with serious cracking in the frames of No.4471, in 1932 Doncaster adopted the practice of welding a new front three-quarters of a strengthened frame on to the back end, now that increased weight was acceptable to the Chief Civil Engineer. Several sets of spare frames were held in stock to avoid detaining engines out of traffic longer than was necessary. Eventually most of the A1 and A3 Pacifics received new front frame sections.

The A3s, like most engine classes, had various devices tried out during their life. Gresley had applied poppet valves with a degree of success, notably to some fifty D49 4-4-0s and ex-Great Central B3 4-6-0s. He took care to ensure that the engines were allocated to a small number of depots where staff were experienced with them. With use of rotary cam poppet valves on No.2001 COCK O' THE NORTH, it is said that some thought had initially been given to fitting the gear to No.2508 BROWN JACK, the last A3. If true, that appears

to have been abandoned at an early stage. Various types of proprietary devices were tried, for Gresley was always open to new ideas and would try those that seemed to offer promise of economy. One was the use of ACFI feed water heating on Nos.2576 THE WHITE KNIGHT and 2580 SHOTOVER, which failed to show any significant saving in fuel.

Following a bad accident on the LMSR in which the driver's ability to see ahead was frustrated by exhaust beating down, exhaust deflection was studied by the big companies. Doncaster tried a number of smokebox arrangements on Nos.2747 CORONACH and 2751 HUMORIST in order to improve smoke deflection and prevent the obscuring of signals in adverse weather conditions. The experiments involved a number of different arrangements retaining the same blastpipe size, using single and double chimneys with and without rims, small deflectors and a sloping smokebox crown. None were found to be satisfactory in service. The experiments seem to have indicated that a sloping smokebox top and small chimneyside deflectors were the best of an unpromising set of arrangements. It was this design that was used for the first two P2s and the A4s, before the streamlined casing was added and found to have overcome the exhaust problems completely. As mentioned before, Gresley lost control of the Running Department at Grouping; such experiments as these were less than enthusiastically applied as a result and less conclusive than they

Haymarket's third new A3, No.2797 CICERO, at her home shed. The date is May 2nd 1931. It always seemed curious that whereas the first two Haymarket A3s, CALL BOY and SPEARMINT were famous for their work on the "Non-stop" in the 1930s, the third was never used or even tried. Boiler: 94A (8248) Tender: Non corridor (5481) W.G. Boyden, Frank Hornby Collection.

King's Cross Top Shed in the 1930s. The A3 is the original GRAND PARADE, and it is probably about to go off shed for the 10.00 departure. It may well have a corridor tender. The background is interesting, too: what is an O2 2-8-0 doing there, I wonder? There is a GE 4-4-0 on the right, and an N7 0-6-2T on the left. Boiler: 94A (unknown) Tender: Probably corridor (5331).

might have been. It was the latter engine, No.2751 HUMORIST, that was chosen for a more important experiment in 1937. Gresley had built the revolutionary high pressure compound Class W1 No.10000 at Darlington and, for reasons which lay outside the scope of this book, No.10000 did not perform as well as was hoped. In 1929 the rebuilding of No.3566 on the PO system in France had astonished the locomotive world. Whereas the power developed by the high pressure cylinders was not increased significantly, that of the low pressure cylinders was trebled, raising the locomotive's total power output to 3,000 IHP. One of the principal improvements in No.3566 was the powerful double blastpipe design evolved by André Chapelon, the Kylala-Chapelon (Kylchap) blastpipe and chimney. The use of this design together with straight and ample steam passages allowed the engine to develop greater power through improved evaporation and lower back pressure.

In 1933 it was thought that the more efficient Kylchap double exhaust and resuperheat would stimulate performance by No.10000 and a design by the Associated Locomotive Equipment Co., Chapelon's agents in the UK, was fitted in 1935. It increased power output by 20%, but not by enough to justify continuing with the experiment. Gresley, through his friendship with M André Chapelon in France, had heard of the Kylchap

exhaust and its successful application to a variety of French locomotives including Pacifics and 4-8-0s, and used it on the Mikados. The W1 No.10000 was later rebuilt as a conventional 4-6-4 with boiler generally similar to the Mikados, and the rebuilt engine was re-equipped with a new Kylchap double exhaust. It was decided that an A3 and a new A4 were also to be fitted, No.2751 being the A3 and No.4468 the A4. The latter was followed by the last three A4s being similarly fitted.

By reason of what was achieved with MALLARD, it is understandable that the A3 and W1 tended to be overlooked. No.2751 was fitted with a Kylchap double chimney in July 1937: it sat well forward in order to clear the superheater header, and was one of a number of minor changes which detracted from the elegance of the early design. The A1s and A3s had carried a number of experimental exhausts. While it seemed that their reliable steaming before the war owed much to skill and hard work, post-war it seemed to be much less reliable. By all accounts No.2751 was a good runner and her performance was enhanced by the double chimney, but we are talking of days when the standard of firing and of fuel was high, and Pacifics did not usually run short of steam. One problem with the softer exhaust was that drivers who worked the engine according to the sound from the chimney tended to be unnecessarily heavy handed. Due to the soft exhaust, No.2751 was fitted with small

chimneyside deflectors in February 1938. No particular effort was made to evaluate the deflectors, which were well-nigh ineffective. In May 1947 large smoke deflectors replaced the small, ineffective ones, and a new chimney with the normal lip was fitted in April 1951 in place of the previous stovepipe.

Much has been made of the naming of the A1s and A3s. A few of the engines carried names such as GREAT NORTHERN, SIR FREDERICK BANBURY, WILLIAM WHITELAW or CENTENARY, but the main theme for naming was the winners of classic horse races. Perhaps it was a Doncastrian inspiration, from the home of the St Leger. One, No.2553, was initially named MANNA but was renamed PRINCE OF WALES two years later to mark a Royal Visit to Doncaster, and its first name was transferred to A3 No.2596. If one was brought up near the East Coast main line, the racehorse names were peculiarly appropriate to steam engines that were very much the iron horse. One thinks of ROYAL LANCER, GALOPIN, NIGHT HAWK or TRIGO. One which had more than a whiff of the stables was actually a highwayman, DICK TURPIN, since no four legged racing equivalent has been found. ROBERT THE DEVIL was famously turned out to haul a special train for a church conference. Those at Doncaster Works were convinced, however, that the engine's name was a joke at the expense of the portly Works

Manager, Robert Thom! However if one came from elsewhere, the names must have seemed at times superb, often quaint and at times ridiculous. What passed without comment in the racing world was not always appropriate for locomotives. Of course it is a matter of taste, but these engines were old friends to many of us who saw them every day. But even I, as one of them, felt that the humble functionary whose task it was to read the horse racing equivalent of Wisden should have had the sense to pass over PRETTY POLLY, SPEARMINT and SALMON TROUT! And of course, important though captains of industry were, their names certainly didn't do much for the engines.

In 1941, when the railways were working as never before to sustain the country's resistance to German air raids, Sir Nigel Gresley died of a heart attack. He was almost 65 and his had been an outstanding career with the GNR and the LNER, and many grieved his passing. He had come to be regarded with something approaching affection by shed and footplate staff, and his locomotives were greatly liked. During the war years, the LNER management had good reason to be glad of the number of large and powerful engines that Gresley had provided.

His successor was Edward Thompson, his assistant as Mechanical Engineer (Southern Area), a man unusually well academically qualified amongst his peers but one whose short tenure of office generated much controversy. The conversion of A10s into A3s accelerated during the war years so that at the end of

Thompson's period of office in 1946 there were few 180psi boilers still in service. As all railway workshops were heavily occupied in producing armaments, this seemed entirely sensible for Doncaster, for there was little capacity for heavy boiler and firebox repairs that could otherwise be avoided, and steel was in short supply A proposal to use the V2 diagram 109 boiler was examined in view of the fact that a large number were being manufactured at the time, but it was not taken up. The shorter boiler was favoured by Thompson, who used it on his own Pacifics.

One A1 was not rebuilt into an A3, and that was No.4470 GREAT NORTHERN herself, which was selected for rebuilding into Edward Thompson's inelegant prototype A1 in 1945. It was a decision that caused much pain among those who loved the graceful lines of the Gresley Pacific both in and out of the industry. On the other hand it always seems to be forgotten that Edward Thompson was without doubt trying to create a genuinely more powerful, reliable and efficient locomotive out of the oldest of Gresley's Pacifics. This happened towards the end of a desperate war, and new building for anything other than mixed traffic and heavy freight types was not allowed. Rebuilding to improve efficiency and reliability was, and obliquely, what was started with No.4470 succeeded, but later in his successor's A1s and not his. As a result of that rebuilding, in 1945 the few remaining Gresley A1s had become reclassified as A10s. The last original Pacific was Carlisle's No.68 SIR VISTO in December 1948.

No.4470 was put back into traffic effectively as a new engine in September 1945 and almost all of the GNR prototype which was usable was consumed in repairing her sisters. It has to be remembered that a locomotive was comprised of many components, which in fact had an existence of their own. A prosaic engineering view, maybe, but an overhauled locomotive in its near pristine condition may well have received a different boiler from that which it had carried on arrival at the works, different wheels and a different tender, as well as having the damaged or worn components scrapped. Much of the original engine had been replaced over the years. No.4470's tender passed to the new No.4470 and the 180psi boiler would in any case have been replaced. It was suggested that perhaps the wheel centres might have been reused, but even the nameplate was new. The old curved plates were placed in the LNER York Museum, and now survive in the National Railway Museum. Nevertheless, for many who loved the elegance and satisfying appearance of Gresley's first Pacific, the idea of the prototype Gresley Pacific, if not the reality, had been violated and for that, Edward Thompson remained unforgiven.

It gradually became clear that the A3s of the immediate post-war years were not the force generally that they were. Their performance was variable. Forty 6ft 2ins Pacifics had joined the Pacific stud, followed by forty-nine 6ft 8ins Peppercorn A1s built at Doncaster and Darlington. These, with Kylchap double chimneys, were freer steaming and more powerful engines. The newly

SHOTOVER, as built, between 1925, and early 1928 when she was fitted with a diagram 94HP 220 psi boiler and long travel valves. She was the shortest-lived A1, being rebuilt as an A3 three years and three months after building. The North British locomotives had the typical works plate on the smokebox and a Darlington type reversing rod, dipped below the Westinghouse pump. They also had the small cabside numberplate, with the LNER initials and number on the tender side. Boiler: 94 (7802) Tender: GN (5290) G. Goslin, The Gresley Society.

WINDSOR LAD on the turntable at Haymarket. Note that the engine has been correctly placed in mid-gear whilst turning. I would estimate the date as between September 1951 and April 1952, probably the first being more likely, given the tell-tale streaks of rust that have not yet been cleaned off. The A3 has been painted green, while A4 No.60011 EMPIRE OF INDIA in the background is still in BR dark blue, which sets the dates. The Peppercorn A1 in the background still has a stovepipe double chimney. Boiler: 94HP (27053) Tender: Non corridor (5567) W. Hermiston, The Transport Treasury.

formed British Railways had introduced the LMSR system of power classification, under which the A3s became 7P. The system was then amended in order to avoid the 5XP "Jubilees" and 6P "Royal Scots" sharing the same status, which clearly they did not. As a result the Peppercorn A1s and the A4s moved up to 8P whilst the A3s, with less than 35,000lb tractive effort, stayed 7P. As locomotive diagrams stated the power classification required, the A3s were effectively relegated from many of the principal duties unless an 8P – an A4 or Peppercorn A1 – was unavailable. From September 1951 to October 1956 they rarely ran through from London to Newcastle, and the old favourites started to look rather old. The A1s and A4s held sway very much at the southern end of the East Coast main line. It was also noticeable that the single blast A3s and A4s were sometimes in difficulties for steam with lower grades of coal and inexperienced firemen.

All design, even the most trifling alteration, was controlled from the British Transport Commission (and later the British Railways Board) and that responsibility was jealously guarded there. Unfortunately those in charge were mainly from the old LMSR who were rather narrow minded and conservative and their efforts were directed towards simple LMS designs which were easy to maintain. They were not prepared to pay much heed to

Doncaster, Eastleigh and Swindon, let alone import ideas from overseas, whether they were valuable or not. A series of experiments started, controlled by Swindon testing staff, trying to improve the single chimney Pacifics' steaming following encouraging results with V2 No.60845 at Swindon Test Plant in 1953.

The CMEE at Doncaster applied the Swindon proportions experimentally to several A3 and A4s to improve steaming with the self-cleaning apparatus in place in the smokebox. Depots had to report periodically through the Regional Motive Power Officer to the CMEE at Doncaster. As the results were difficult to measure no conclusive improvement was established. The redoubtable Eastern Region Motive Power Officer, L.P. Parker, prompted by Peter Townend, observed that all that was needed was to re-draught the single chimney locomotives with the Kylchap exhaust system that worked faultlessly with those locomotives so fitted. Gresley had appreciated the value of a powerful exhaust in stimulating a greater rate of evaporation, but hitherto the Kylchap equipment had to be bought and the royalties paid. Nevertheless before his death the need for royalty payments was about to pass, and Sir Nigel had issued an instruction that all future construction of large locomotives should include a Kylchap exhaust. Edward Thompson also knew the value

of the Kylchap and incorporated it in his Pacifics. Arthur Peppercorn did not, and handicapped fourteen of his fifteen A2s as a result.

The CMEE, K.J. Cook, an ex-GWR man, ignored this advice and persisted in applying the Swindon proportions for some years. Suffice it to say that the engines became extremely noisy through the greater back pressure and longer cut-offs used as a result. The volume of half burnt coal dust ejected from the chimney was considerable: as far as steaming was concerned it made only some slight improvement. The A3s, working hard, had a fine impressive roar from the chimney normally, but now the modified engines were deafening when working hard.

In 1954 it was decided to stop producing Diagram 94A boilers, and to fit Diagram 107 A4 boilers to A3s, working at 220 psi, instead of Diagram 94A or 94HP. Hudd automatic train control had been tried experimentally before the war in Scotland and, post-war, Automatic Train Control equipment (later renamed Automatic Warning System) was provided on a number of engines initially working between Barnet and Huntingdon. AWS and speed indicators were fitted more generally in the late 1950s. Located under the buffer beam, the AWS receiver necessitated the removal of bogie dust shields that had become a very characteristic part of the appearance of the front of an A3.

K.J. Cook had spent much of his

time concerned with Swindon Works and had brought a Great Western workshop mind to bear on the old LNER and its engineering practices. Cook used the opportunity to bring modern engineering practices into steam locomotive maintenance and overhaul. One of the innovations he brought was the use of Zeiss optical equipment, used at Swindon to align the frames, axleboxes and cylinders. The frame of a Gresley Pacific can be flex considerably since the concentrated drive restricts the extent of any frame bracing around the central driving axle. At the front end of course the closely aligned cylinder castings of a Gresley engine provide much more strength, as compared with the Thompson Pacifics with divided drive. Whilst the optical system achieved a great deal of tightening up generally, it meant that each engine overhauled would have an unique set of driving axleboxes to accommodate individual dimensions. Overhauled locomotives were despatched with a spare set on board. In the confusion that followed the replacement axleboxes were sometimes transposed left and right, but the engines were unaffected. The frames of the Gresley Pacifics were subjected to greater flexure than the more rigid and thicker frame structure of the GWR 4-6-0s, for which the optical lining-up system was originally installed.

Simultaneously with the use of the optical equipment, Cook introduced smaller tolerances which were essential in automotive and particularly in diesel traction. Bearings were re-engineered and features such as the middle big end became an accurately machined continuous white metal bearing with

clearances of the order of 8-9 thousandths of an inch, contributing to better, quieter running than hitherto. In order to keep weight down, Gresley had used high strength nickel chrome steel in the motion of his Pacifics which, with the tolerances used at Doncaster, gave a characteristic ringing sound to the locomotives – the "Gresley Knock". It was probably due to side clearances rather than a true "knock". It was once said, unkindly and indeed incorrectly, that Doncaster's tolerances when new were what Swindon would scrap. Embrittlement fractures occurred in the connecting rods, and carbon steel, introduced as a wartime economy, became the normal replacement. Slowly the sound of the "Gresley Knock" disappeared as the nickel chrome steel was replaced and bearings ran more quietly.

The overhauled locomotives, without the familiar sounds from the motion, sounded quite different. O.S. Nock collaborated with Bishop Eric Treacy in producing a superb book "Main Lines across the Border", and part of his experiences quoted was a footplate trip with No.60095 FLAMINGO. Nock was quite confounded by the A3, which rode "like a ghost machine" over the very taxing Waverley route, pulling strongly and sounding unlike any that he had experienced before.

I remember a similar experience travelling southbound in 1957 from Grantham on the 17.15 from Leeds. It was the heaviest train of the day, fifteen coaches weighing 550 tons or more with its usual complement of passengers, and it was a summer Saturday. The A3 that took over at Grantham was No.60103 FLYING SCOTSMAN, much to my surprise, as

it was just ex-Works from Doncaster, still of course, a single blast locomotive. Hardly a light running in turn! As the train accelerated up the hill to Stoke the sound of the engine was quite unlike any A3 that I had heard before. The valves had been set by a genius, for the exhaust was even, like an LM Region "Jubilee", and of course, gone was the "Gresley Knock", which had characterised the class. No.60103 reached 86mph down the hill to Peterborough in comparative silence and after restarting powerfully we ran well over Stilton Fen. There was a 20mph temporary speed restriction (TSR) at Sandy, and yet the 34 year old engine accelerated this big train up to 60-70mph within a few miles, the sound of her exhaust music to the ears. Technical opinions are not always unanimous but the quality of valve-setting at Doncaster Works was regarded by many engineers as being of the highest standard.

With the October winter timetable in 1956, maximum train loads were cut and accelerated services run more frequently. In 1957, tests were carried out on the A3s with a dynamometer car to ascertain whether they could work the "Talisman" not with its usual 8 coach load but strengthened by 3-4 coaches on Fridays. I saw Nos.60054 and 60055 and the two engines seemed to be running well. Nos.60060 and 60073 from Gateshead were also involved. As a result, although most of the duties were diagrammed for 8P locomotives, the A3s started to work turn and turn about with the A4s and Peppercorn A1s when necessary on most trains between London and Newcastle. With lighter loads and a reduced demand for steam, the A3s could fly as of old, and drivers preferred

BLINK BONNY seems to have acclimatised to life at Neasden by the look of her external condition. She is climbing the 1 in 164 from High Wycombe to Saunderton with the down "Master Cutler" past Bradenham village, on May 31st 1951. The A3 is still right-hand drive, and despite the banjo dome trying to look like a simple dome, it is in fact a diagram 94A boiler. Boiler: 94A (27013) Tender: GN (5260).

No.60037 HYPERION waiting on the up Aberdeen line in Princes Street Gardens at Edinburgh. When the driver got a green aspect he would have taken the A3 into Waverley on to her train. The BR blue livery sets the date between June 1950 and March 1952. The driver had more than a passing likeness to Norman McKillop: his fireman seemed to have a dusty tenderful to make steam with but seemed to be managing well enough. Boiler: 94A (27072) Tender: GN (5285) J. Robertson, The Transport Treasury.

A locomotive freshly overhauled and repainted was a vision to behold. Three days after leaving the Works, on January 30th 1955, MERRY HAMPTON was just across the town in Doncaster shed. One can almost smell the new paint and it still looks wet! Boiler: 94A (27044) Tender: GN (5223) B.K.B. Green, Initial Photographics.

their smooth riding to the livelier if more powerful Peppercorn A1s, given the choice.

In May of that year the first conversion of a single blast A4, No.60017 SILVER FOX to Kylchap double blast was completed, something for which many inside the industry and outside had waited so long. Peter Townend, on being appointed to King Cross depot, had made a firm proposal for conversion of the single chimney A4s, then the A3s. The proposal was supported by trials establishing the saving in fuel. The expenditure was authorised by the Eastern Region management to the CMEE and the re-draughting implemented, first on the A4s and then the A3s. So, in June 1958, No.60055 WOOLWINDER emerged from Doncaster fitted with a Kylchap double chimney, despite being over thirty years old. The converted A3 ran superbly, as many were certain that she would, although there were some on BR who felt, for various reasons, that all the expense and bother were unnecessary at this late stage in the life of steam traction. The conversion was swiftly carried out on the rest of the class, and the Kylchap A3s gained a reputation for free steaming and increased power output arising from reduced back pressure that bore no comparison with past performance, even in the days of the 1930s.

Drifting exhaust had reappeared as a handicap, and after an experiment with the 1938 chimneyside deflectors – still very ineffective – on a number of A3s, German style smoke deflectors were fitted to No.60049 GALTEE MORE. These proved to be very effective, and were fitted to the fifty-five members of the class still in operation. The four A3s at Carlisle Canal received neither AWS nor deflectors and were withdrawn early. One A3, No.60075 ST. FRUSQUIN, of Gateshead shed, was overhauled and by an oversight the deflectors were omitted. They spoilt the appearance of the A3 without doubt, but one had to accept that on a working railway, safety is paramount. Drifting exhaust, especially in certain wind conditions, can prevent a driver observing the signals. The exhaust beating down from a double chimney, especially as later fitted with a rim, can blank out all forward vision, and at high speed that is extremely dangerous, as I have seen myself many times.

By this time however, the older engines were approaching forty years old. New diesel locomotives were coming in, the famous premise being that 22 Deltics would replace 55 steam engines. The Deltics themselves were obviously expensive machines, and their true cost was not widely known for several years. Their enormous power and reliability relative to steam traction made them formidable replacements, and one could see that the end was in sight for steam. It was not achieved for some years, and I remember Colin Morris, DMPS at King's Cross Division, complaining that of the first forty new D1500s he had received, only four were fit for passenger work. However, a huge investment had been made and the steam fleet had to be sacrificed as a cost saving justifying that investment.

For several years however, the Gresley and other East Coast Pacifics effectively covered non-available diesels and diesel failures, in some cases working intensive diesel diagrams as the need arose. Numerous examples occurred of steam locomotives amassing mileages far more quickly than previously had been the case. For example the 10.00 from Kings Cross would be worked to Newcastle by a Pacific which, after a few hours' servicing, would return with an up express reaching King's Cross at 22.00 or so. Shortly after cleaning the fire it could well be off to Leeds on another return trip. If the diesel locomotive, usually a Type 4, was operable but the train heating had failed, a steam locomotive was coupled inside for train heating. The stronger draught from the Kylchap exhaust had virtually eliminated the need for boiler tube cleaning, and the thinner fire could be cleaned and the engine serviced much more quickly.

Many engines had passed into old age over the years, but it was a shock when in December 1959 the old favourite No.60104 SOLARIO was withdrawn after a collision near Ardsley. Ironically another A3, No.60089 FELSTEAD, running in after repair, was also damaged at the same time, so presumably one was condemned and one was salvaged out of what remained usable. A trickle became a torrent, and by 1965 only four remained. SALMON TROUT and SPEARMINT went in 1965, and PRINCE PALATINE survived until January 1966.

One remained, and that is the one mentioned in the preface which had been sold to Mr. Alan Pegler in January 1963 – the world famous No.4472 FLYING SCOTSMAN. The history of that one engine has filled at least two books already and will no doubt fill another, and there are many things that have been done and many places where the surviving A3 has been. It would have been good to have one or two of the old favourites to remind what a handsome thing an express engine was, but at least we have one to treasure. May FLYING SCOTSMAN run many more miles for our delight.

No.60066 MERRY HAMPTON in her final form, in the last few weeks at Top Shed, May 5th 1963. The famous old place was closed in June 1963. In order to prevent any further use and to eradicate all traces of the railway that had served well and faithfully for over a century, the demolition contractors moved in within the week! Boiler: 107 (29314) Tender: GN (5266) Peter Groom.

A famous picture of an immaculate No.4474 VICTOR WILD, as yet unnamed, leaving Paddington with the 10.30 "Cornish Riviera Express". Boiler: 94 (7695) Tender: GN (5225) G. Goslin, The Gresley Society.

CHAPTER THREE
THE PACIFICS AT WORK

The Gresley A1s, when new, were a forward leap in more than design. We are of course looking back nearly 80 years, when the railway was very different. Doncaster men came no further south than Peterborough. Grantham had established itself as a vital part of the East Coast operations and King's Cross shed had no turntable long enough for the Pacifics until 1924. The London based locomotives had to turn at Hornsey for the time being. The first twelve Great Northern Pacifics were shared between King's Cross, Grantham and Doncaster. Doncaster had the lion's share of the first twelve engines and King's Cross only had two, Nos.4474 and 4475, which was strange considering Doncaster had only two diagrams to London.

The effects of such large locomotives and tenders with greater coal and water capacity were far reaching in their sphere of action and in their haulage ability, their size and tenders allowing them to work far heavier loads over longer distances at greater speeds. On the operational railway, expresses were far less frequent than today, and those that ran were generally heavy. While the four track sections were less congested, they had to negotiate a dense network of slow moving unbraked freight trains almost everywhere throughout the system. At busy periods it was common practice to duplicate or even triplicate the main expresses. At peak periods some expresses were split into as many as six parts. Provision was made in the working timetables of the day for relief paths, details being advertised at the stations. In LNER days the details of excursions were displayed on the printed notice on the smokebox door, but post-war the locomotive simply carried the relief train number at the upper or lower central lamp iron.

The Pacifics operated initially between York and King's Cross, but with the grouping they were tested for possible operation on the Great Central from London as far as Manchester. As mentioned earlier, No.1481 was tested over the North Eastern and North British lines to Edinburgh and Glasgow. In addition there were the various diversionary routes for Sunday engineering possessions or operating needs in extremis, via Cambridge, Lincoln and the New Line through Hertford North. After Grouping Gorton Works was used quite often for running-in. Access to Leeds from the south remained the preserve of the Ivatt Atlantics and K3s, due to weight restrictions on the viaduct at Wakefield. Likewise, apart from the diversionary routes, all other routes to the east of the main line were barred to the Pacifics.

The approach to Liverpool Street precluded the A1s on the grounds of weight and size, which was particularly unfortunate as they would have revolutionised the Great Eastern main line passenger services. As Pacifics were allowed as far into London as Bethnal Green, and RA7 and K3 classes were allowed into Liverpool Street, the problem seemed to be one of weight restriction, not rolling stock gauge, on the bank approaching the terminus. There were distinct boundaries between the technical and operating departments well after the disappearance of steam, and I suspect that this had a lot to do with the reluctance to question the technical departments closely. A weak bridge or two might have been rebuilt and the GE Section transformed as a result.

Admittedly the GER was not a robustly constructed railway, even on the main line, and on its many branch lines the railway was little more than a track laid across the countryside. Moreover, East Anglia was distinctly rural and not the substantial passenger market that it is today, and the LNER was not a wealthy company. The aftermath of the Second World War was pivotal in transforming a rural and sparsely populated area into the commuters' dormitory that it has become. Another quarter of a century had to pass before Pacific power eventually came, in the shape of Bulleid lightweight Pacifics initially, then the BR Standard Britannias. The

The up "Queen of Scots" Pullman at Doncaster, hauled by CENTENARY, one of the two A1s allocated to Copley Hill specially for this duty. The date given is 1938/9. Boiler: 94 (7792) Tender: GN (5257).

A down express climbs the 1 in 105 of Holloway bank behind DIAMOND JUBILEE. The photograph is taken from the up goods line, which is rising to cross over the four passenger lines. The date lies between the building of the A1 in August 1924 and 1928 when numbers were transferred to the cab side. The A1 was not modified with long travel valves until 1931. In those days track, if not actually ballasted with ash, had an ash infill to give a flat surface in and around the tracks. Boiler: 94 (7763) Tender: GN (probably 5255) G. Goslin, The Gresley Society.

GER had been upgraded by then through improved underbridge strength and modern track. In BR days the size and weight of Britannias and Bulleid lightweight Pacifics permitted into the terminus suggested that there had been little to prohibit the A1s that could not have been overcome.

Of those locomotives built at North British, ten went to Gateshead, five to Heaton and five to Haymarket. At the time of grouping the operation of the Newcastle-Edinburgh main line was much more in the hands of the NER sheds than the NB, and Haymarket had a lesser role compared with

Gateshead and Heaton, as reflected in their allocation. Newcastle crews had even formed part of the Haymarket top link as well as at their own depot, having the necessary road knowledge, prior to Grouping.

As the LNER became established the A1s took over express work

An interesting 1923-25 shot of the then unnamed ROYAL LANCER at Ganwick with the up 15.40 mail train. The A1 had L&NER on the tender, but retained a GNR number without a suffix. The train, as in such pictures, is a coach man's delight. It is also interesting because in the distance one can see Ganwick box, which disappeared in about 1932 along with Hadley Wood to the south and Mimms Hall to the north. Ganwick was – and is still – a famous location but only became well known after the signalbox giving it the name had been eliminated. Boiler: 94 (7697) Tender: GN (5227) G. Goslin, The Gresley Society.

No.2566 LADAS stands in the unmistakable surroundings of Edinburgh Waverley station. The date is merely stated as 'pre-war', but the non-corridor tender puts it at after 1930. The presence of an electric ground signal suggests that it would be 1938-39. LADAS was the first conversion to A3 in 1939, after the initial batch of five in 1927-28. Boiler: 94 (7773) Tender: Non-corridor (5479).

generally from London to Aberdeen and Glasgow. Apart from the East Coast main line they operated into Leeds from the north via Ripon and Harrogate, occasionally over the GCR and over diversionary routes as engineering work dictated. The Waverley and the Newcastle-Carlisle routes had been cleared although the trial with No.2563 was the first use of an A1 over the former. The Aberdeen route was cleared as far as Montrose using Gateshead's 220psi No.2573 HARVESTER in 1928, although it was two further years before the LMSR had carried out the necessary strengthening works on their line from Kinnaber Junction to Aberdeen. Later the Perth route via Kinross with its notorious southbound climb to Glenfarg at 1 in 75 was cleared for the operation of Pacifics. The NE Area engines were very occasionally used to Scarborough and Hull but not on a regular basis, and not on the direct route but via Pilmoor and Gilling. Neither Scarborough nor Hull could turn the Pacifics, and later the triangle at Bridlington was used. Pacifics started to work the "Flying Scotsman" between King's Cross and York in 1924. Once confidence was established, the engines started to work longer diagrams, with all three GN depots involved in the running between London and York.

The North Eastern Area was longer in taking to the Pacifics, and Gresley had to meet the crews and deal with their complaints. However, within two-three years attitudes rapidly changed and Gateshead and Heaton were protesting at the temporary loss of their best locomotives for "Non-stop" work! Tyneside A1s worked south to York and then Grantham, and north to Edinburgh. As the LNER moved to longer route distance diagrams, locomotives would work farther afield, and Tyneside and London locomotives began to run throughout in 1927. The five Scottish A1s worked mainly between Glasgow, Edinburgh and Newcastle.

After 1930 they worked to Aberdeen, when the A3s began to arrive in numbers. By then they also worked to Perth. They were far bigger locomotives than Scots crews were familiar with, and learning to handle such a powerful locomotive, and to fire to such a relatively large grate, although not difficult, took time to master. The North British Railway bequeathed the LNER track that was at best ordinary. At worst it was frankly bad, weak, and beset with severe curvature. Between the Firths of Forth and Tay lay the Fife coalfield, and not only was the route restricted in speed because of curvature, but to protect the underground workings from

subsidence or worse. The Pacifics were of course miles above anything north of the Border in size and power, and no doubt the drivers had to exercise caution especially where the track was not robust.

With the introduction of the "Non-stop" in 1928 it was originally proposed to use Gateshead and King's Cross crews since they possessed the necessary route knowledge. Three NE Area engines were sent to Haymarket to operate the service, Nos.2569, 2573 and 2580 being selected. It was significant that two had the higher pressure 220psi boiler. In retrospect this decision was decidedly questionable. It was perhaps excusable bearing in mind the minor role played by Haymarket prior to 1928, but it seems to have been taken overlooking the fact that Haymarket had their own Pacifics. The decision was undermined firstly by a change of plan bringing the Scots crews and engines into the operation, and secondly by the fact that the Newcastle Pacifics had Westinghouse as well as vacuum brakes and both the Haymarket ones and the new corridor tenders had only vacuum. The RCTS *Locomotives of the LNER* sets out the amazing muddle in detail.

No.2569 GLADIATEUR, Gateshead's favourite, was nominated for loan to Haymarket; released only

The up "Flying Scotsman" headed by No.2573 HARVESTER, assisted by ex NER D20 4-4-0 No.2107. There is little to date the shot beyond the conversion of No.2573 in 1928 and the onset of war in 1939. The coupling of the assisting engine inside the train engine enabled the driver of the latter to keep control of the brakes, and also to take first dip at the troughs. The view is from that famous vantage point, the castle east of Central station. Boiler: 94A (number unknown) Tender: GN (5283) G. Goslin, The Gresley Society.

grudgingly, it was soon returned to Gateshead unused. One can imagine the wrath of Gateshead, having lost two good engines, on receiving as replacement No.2565, a vacuum-only engine and then having their favourite returned unused but also now vacuum-only! In retrospect it is surprising since although No.2569 was the only 180 psi engine of the three, she had just been given a general repair and was fitted with long travel valves, and King's Cross and Haymarket had no qualms about using 180 psi locomotives on the "Non-stop". On the first day however, Heaton's 220 psi A1 No.2580 SHOTOVER worked the first up "Non-stop" and 180 psi A1 No.4472 FLYING SCOTSMAN worked the down train. On the third day King's Cross had to substitute No.2546 DONOVAN with a corridor tender since one of No.4472's tender axleboxes had overheated and needed repair. The 'Scottish' A3, SHOTOVER, had carried a Flying Scotsman headboard on the inaugural run, and this was enthusiastically received by the LNER management, so much so that the London engine was similarly decorated. Headboards were adopted for the other named trains of the LNER.

The "Non-stop" was operated successfully by A1s and A3s from 1928 until 1936. In 1928 King's Cross used A1s, Nos.2547 DONCASTER and 4476 ROYAL LANCER with No.4472, with No.2552 SANSOVINO in reserve. Haymarket used No.2573 HARVESTER with No.2580 initially. Then their own A1s Nos.2563 WILLIAM WHITELAW and 2564 KNIGHT OF THE THISTLE were coupled to corridor tenders and took over, later joined by Nos.2565 MERRY HAMPTON and 2566 LADAS. In successive summers the new A3s took part in the "Non-stop" working. Most of the first batch of ten A3s were coupled to corridor tenders for a while, including even the Carlisle engines, before they gravitated to the chosen engines at King's Cross and Haymarket. At the latter shed Nos.2795 CALL BOY, 2796 SPEARMINT and 2508 BROWN JACK were used with A1s Nos.2563 and 2564, while No.2506 SALMON TROUT was held as a reserve before the A4s took over in 1937.

King's Cross continued to use A1s 2547, 4472 and 4476 but these were joined by a variety of engines including the famous No.2750 PAPYRUS, No.2746 FAIRWAY and other early A3s. Gateshead should not be forgotten, for it was their favourite No.2569 which ran 55 consecutive cyclic diagrams including King's Cross and Edinburgh with the down "Flying Scotsman" in the winter of 1929. Over the years the A1s and A3s of the North Eastern Area of the LNER worked hard and reliably. In those days it became quite commonplace for locomotives to work between York and Edinburgh as part of a longer diagram. In post-war years, locomotives were always changed at Newcastle, the "Non-stop" being the only exception. An interesting feature of the summer working timetable in the 1930s was that Pacifics worked through between King's Cross and Edinburgh from the beginning of May to the end of September and not just for the duration of the "Non-stop", which was mid-June to mid September. Thus the Pacifics coupled to non-corridor tenders could share in the work, and even those with GN tenders with capacity for eight tons of coal instead of nine. That would have been extremely tight if not impossible with the original valve design. Over the years to 1936 a total 26 engines worked the train, some briefly and some extensively. In 1937, apart from a return trip on the 6th and 7th August by No.2750, the "Non-stop" was taken over by the A4s, and an era finished.

In Scotland Pacifics started to displace the Reid Atlantics on the heaviest duties over the difficult Edinburgh-Aberdeen route from 1928 onwards. Hitherto, they had worked between Glasgow and Newcastle. The A1s and A3s were capable of hauling all but the very heaviest loads over this difficult route, although the line between the Firths of Forth and Tay was plagued with both heavy curvature and permanent speed restrictions as mentioned above. They had to traverse the single track from Usan signalbox over the South Esk bridge to Montrose, a hard pull southbound, and No.2567 SIR VISTO was fitted at Cowlairs Works with an automatic tablet catcher as an experiment. After 1930 several of the A1s were moved to Dundee Tay Bridge and similarly equipped.

The Aberdeen route had a few heavy trains, chief among them being the "Aberdonian", since it was a popular holiday route, but it was heavily graded in places. The Scottish quintet worked from Haymarket shed originally, but as more locomotives were allocated they moved around to Eastfield, Dundee Tay Bridge and Aberdeen Ferryhill, and also St. Margarets. There seemed to be little rhyme or reason other than to provide a large locomotive or two for a particularly heavy duty, since their allowed loading was 30% higher than for a Reid Atlantic.

After the trials with Nos.2563 and 2580, some of the new A3s were allocated to Carlisle Canal in order to work the Waverley route, which ran from Carlisle to Edinburgh. The line carried a few but important expresses, a few semi-fast stopping services and fast and local freight. The loading of some expresses had escalated beyond the capacity of a Reid Atlantic. The crucial point was that the services were a link between the Midlands and Northern cities and the Scottish capital, and it was important for the company to be seen to be offering a reliable and competitive service. The overnight services were especially important. However, it was a very difficult line to operate, hardly a main line at all by East Coast standards. It crossed remote country, with much curvature and was very heavily graded even by Scottish standards, with no opportunity for speed to make use of those 6ft 8ins coupled wheels.

Most of the first batch went to Southern Area sheds but two new A3s were allocated to Carlisle Canal in 1928/29, Nos.2745 CAPTAIN CUTTLE and 2749 FLAMINGO plus No.4480 ENTERPRISE. Several of the new A3s including the two for Carlisle were initially allocated to Doncaster, but for no more than running-in. No.4480, surprisingly, was not popular, possibly because her larger 20in cylinders made her much more susceptible to wheelslip. Her factor of adhesion was 15% less than an A3 and she was replaced by No.2748 COLORADO from Top Shed. Apart from her initial weeks at Doncaster running in, No.2749 was remarkable in spending her entire working life at Carlisle. There seems to have been some uncertainty at the time of building as to where each engine was being allocated, for both Nos.2745 and 2749 were coupled to corridor tenders as mentioned earlier. No.2749 left her corridor tender at Doncaster on transfer, but No.2745 retained hers, possibly since the Carlisle engine stood alongside the "Non-stop" at Waverley on a 10.05 Edinburgh to Carlisle and St. Pancras train and could be used in extremis. Be that as it may, the tender was swapped with No.2796 at Haymarket in 1930.

From Carlisle Nos.2745, 2748 and 2749 worked to Edinburgh on loads up to 400 tons and occasionally to Newcastle on semi-fast services. In view of the lighter nature of the permanent way, together with the low speeds – for an express engine – on the severe and lengthy gradients of the Waverley route, the use of so large and heavy an engine as the A3 seemed unwise. Remembering Gresley's predilection for small groups of a specialist design, one wonders what he might have produced. However the reason for their use, despite the 6ft 8ins coupled wheels, was their tractive effort of just under 33,000lb and their adhesive weight, which was similar to the V2s that later performed with distinction on this road. This and their greater boiler capacity were far in excess of the K3 2-6-0 which already worked over this road, or even the Raven B16 4-6-0 from the North Eastern Area which did not, but might have been considered. I suppose the ideal engine for this road came 25 years later in the shape of the BR 9F

SANDWICH at Kings Cross, waiting to depart on May 9th 1959; a month later she went into Doncaster for a general overhaul. The A3s carried small BR works plates at the front of their frames during BR ownership but Doncaster kept the originals as well. The A3 is coupled to her non-corridor tender No.5573, which she kept throughout her career. Boiler: 94A (27014) Bryan Wilson, The Transport Treasury.

2-10-0, with greater adhesion and a coupled wheelbase 50% longer than an A3, although the Pacific's leading bogie was more suitable as a vehicle than the pony truck of the 9F. However, theory is all very fine; in the event the Carlisle men took to their A3s, and this was yet another demonstration that the steam engine is nothing if not adaptable. Later in 1940, No.2567 SIR VISTO made it a quartet. With No.2749 she remained there, the last Gresley 180 psi A10 to be rebuilt in 1948, until the end of steam, joined by BR No.60079 BAYARDO (2578) and LNER No. 2747 CORONACH in place of Nos.2745 and 2748.

Grantham and New England enjoyed considerable rivalry in the 1930s, Grantham usually getting better of it. Grantham of course was a passenger shed with a number of fast fish freights, while New England was largely concerned with freight, although it also powered a number of semi-fasts – "Parleys" as they were universally known. Indeed New England was widely known as "Bungett" to the GN cognoscenti, for reasons lost in history. The fleet of A1s at Grantham was kept in superb condition mechanically and outwardly. They worked some of the turns from King's Cross through to York, from and to Grantham before and after the York return trip, which totalled over 750 miles per diagram. Doncaster shed, "Carr Loco", worked

many of the West Riding and Hull trains to and from London before Pacifics were allowed into Leeds via Wakefield. One of the fastest trains was the 7.50 from Leeds Central, unofficially known as the "Breakfast Flyer". One of the outstanding engines on this duty was No.2544 with her regular driver, Charlie Molson, who frequently exceeded 90mph down Stoke bank.

The first batch having gone to the Southern area and Carlisle, the next batch of five A3s, Nos.2595-2599, went to Gateshead shed and remained in the NE Area throughout their careers, except for No.2598 BLENHEIM which moved to Haymarket. Nos.2795-2797 for some reason were built in the middle of the batch, all going to Haymarket. These were Haymarket's first A3s, and Nos.2795 and 2796 distinguished themselves on the "Non-stop" as mentioned earlier. Curiously, the third engine, No.2797 CICERO, remained one of the most elusive of the class south of the Tyne. The 1934/35 batch was sent exclusively to Gateshead and Haymarket where they remained until No.2504 SANDWICH came south from Gateshead to King's Cross in exchange for the third new A4, No.2511 SILVER KING. The latter was then available to act as pilot for the "Silver Jubilee" service, also working to York and Edinburgh.

No. 2500 WINDSOR LAD was a great favourite at Haymarket, the regular engine of Bill Stevenson, and accumulated a high mileage with few stoppages. There was a good-natured rivalry between the top drivers as to whose engine was the best, as nearly always happened when men and locomotives were regularly paired. On one occasion Bill Stevenson's A3 had reached the shed having run hot between Dunbar and Edinburgh, the reason was found to be a missing tyre. The tyre had split into two – probably more, and been thrown clear. It was fortunate, for a serious derailment could well have resulted. The batch of tyres was traced and replaced as a matter of urgency. Fellow Haymarket driver Norman McKillop wrote for several magazines including a trade union journal under the name "Toram Beg". His regular engine was No.2796, later BR No.60100 SPEARMINT, and those who read his anecdotes understood the close relationship between man and machine. Norman also drew attention to the fact that sister engine No.2502 HYPERION at one time was widely regarded as a bad runner at Haymarket. The locomotive's valve timing was found to be wrong, and with attention and adjustment the engine's performance was corrected. It is a curious thing that otherwise identical locomotives can be so different in performance, and the bad

No.60039 SANDWICH at the head of a down express at Hadley Wood in dull weather. The hoarding proclaimed the long awaited widening project, started in 1954. The first vehicle appears to be an old GER coach, strong on interest if weak on comfort! The famous "bottleneck" actually extended from New Barnet station to north of Potters Bar station for passenger trains, the extra down line being the down goods, i.e. freight only. It was a tremendous obstacle for many years and was only finally overcome in May 1959. Boiler: 94A (probably 27057) Tender: Non-corridor (5573) The Transport Treasury.

reputation can survive even after a general overhaul in which the major components are replaced. Whether this says more about the traditionalism of footplate crews than bad steaming or running is a moot point.

Bridge strengthening on the Calder viaduct started in 1930 and the Chief Civil Engineer allowed one Pacific into Leeds each weekday until work was complete in 1936, when Copley Hill shed received two A1s. The use of No.4472 on the high speed test in 1934 marked a change in operating policy. It was significant that it was an A1 and not an A3, a slightly heavier locomotive. The Pacifics were still not allowed the use of the LMSR metals at Wakefield in emergency diversions. The Atlantics at Leeds (Copley Hill) were replaced on the "Queen of Scots" Pullman by Nos.2553 PRINCE OF WALES and 2555 CENTENARY in late 1936. This was also partly because the proposed streamlined service planned for Leeds needed an acceptable substitute should the A4 fail. An Ivatt

No.60037 HYPERION at Craigentinny on June 8th 1957. She has brought empty stock from Waverley by the look of the headcode. The first coach was a late Gresley non-corridor, a handsome vehicle for a short run, but on some strange non-Gresley bogies. The right-hand coach is a twelve wheeler, an uncommon sight on the East Coast main line. Boiler: 94A (27027) Tender: GN (5276) J. Robertson, The Transport Treasury.

No.60087 BLENHEIM, at the head of a down Aberdeen express, running through Princes Street Gardens at Edinburgh, June 20th 1959. If the photographer wanted clouds of billowing exhaust, the double chimney was not a lot of help as can be seen here. Boiler: 94A (27006) Tender: Non-corridor (5572) J. Robertson, The Transport Treasury.

Atlantic was not an acceptable option, though no doubt a keen crew could always surprise! Post-war, A3s and Peppercorn A1s were allocated to Copley Hill until September 1957, when the A3 fleet was moved to Gateshead.

One of the features of pre-war operation which drew particular attention from the enthusiast fraternity was the growing appeal of soccer. The Cup Finals for amateur and professional clubs attracted huge numbers as did the Cup tie matches, and the England-Scotland 'international' matches were far more important in the public mind than today. As a result, numbers of special trains were laid on that brought some strange visitors to the capital, and the older enthusiasts dined out on their recollections. Rising at unthinkable hours, they were rewarded by unusual visitors which would not normally be seen. The sights of NE Atlantics, D49s and Pacifics were recalled, and before the 1939-45 war the Scottish Pacifics occasionally worked through to King's Cross with football specials, something which was almost unknown after the war. The Pacifics were, of course, remanned en route. Something of a climax was reached in 1934, when a late friend noted LADAS and SIR VISTO from not merely Haymarket shed but Tay Bridge at Dundee, and no

less than the fabled CAPTAIN CUTTLE, borrowed from Carlisle Canal! In the post-war years such through workings by the larger engines had become a thing of the past, and locomotives kept to their own Area, or later, Region, much more.

Heaton's A3s were not common visitors beyond Grantham but came much more into the picture in the mid-1930s and during the war, when Gateshead transferred Pacifics there as the new A4s arrived. The A3s joined the A1s in working long diagrams that took them to Edinburgh and Glasgow in the north and to London in the south. Before the war the "Queen of Scots" Pullman was worked between Leeds and Edinburgh without changing engines. Post-war the Neville Hill A3s, which only worked northwards and never south until the 1960s, worked only to Newcastle on the "Queen of Scots" and "North Briton" services. In the late 1930s Nos.2580 SHOTOVER and 2597 GAINSBOROUGH were sent to Leeds Neville Hill for a short period, and another larger batch went there in 1945. In September 1949 they received their original pair plus three more, Nos.60036 COLOMBO, 60074 HARVESTER and 60084 TRIGO, to work services northwards to Newcastle and Edinburgh via York or Ripon.

My earliest memories are as a small boy, visiting my grandmother,

who had the presence of mind to live by Ferme Park Yard between Harringay and Hornsey, and also to own an ancient pair of binoculars. The main line could be watched from the high amphitheatre of the footpath above Ferme Park South Down signalbox, or from her house. From among the dozens of small tank engines of Class J52, the "Coffee Pots", the bigger locomotives could be seen, and in their midst were the expresses. The condition of locomotives during and after the war was filthy, and one looked for a nameplate that would establish the identity of the locomotive. Such memories fade slowly but among the many names such as ROBERT THE DEVIL, SANDWICH and TRACERY there were the less common visitors from Tyneside – GLADIATEUR, GALOPIN, NIGHT HAWK and NEIL GOW. There were a few rare visitors such as COLORADO and WINDSOR LAD, which I never saw since south of Doncaster. The lack of a nameplate indicated that the locomotive was a V2, which was always something of an anti-climax. After the war blue and green engines started to re-appear, and then there was the confusion – for a small boy – of the renumbering system which brought a sensible reordering to what had existed before. We were heavily dependent on the early Ian Allan ABCs in those days, especially when confronted with new and unknown numbers.

In May 1948 No.60091 CAPTAIN CUTTLE was painted, unaccountably, in an experimental dark purple livery, but once Authority realised that few would see her on the Waverley route, she was sent to Heaton in exchange for No.60079 BAYARDO, much to the incredulous delight of lineside enthusiasts. The four Carlisle A3s were very rare visitors to the capital, as were the residents of Neville Hill and Haymarket, too! At the halfway mark through the century, the number of duties between London and Newcastle increased, and many old Tyneside favourites became commonplace visitors. Not only did Gateshead have turns to London, but Heaton too, including the "Tees-Tyne Pullman" initially, until May 1949 when King's Cross took over the diagram. They also worked the up Newcastle and Saltburn express arriving at about 13.35 and returned on the 17.35 King's Cross-Newcastle. I had begun to learn about allocations, and the difference between depots, and watching the 17.35 after school, Heaton's fleet of Pacifics became a more familiar sight in North London. Whereas Gateshead concentrated more on using their new Peppercorn A1s, Heaton had only three, and although Nos.60116, 60126 and 60127 were frequent sights, we eagerly waited for

the 17.35 to see a gleaming A3, often Nos.60072 SUNSTAR or 60077 THE WHITE KNIGHT which were frequent performers on this turn. Nearly all express engines at that time had BR blue livery, and Heaton kept theirs spotlessly clean.

There was a presence then in the major services that we have lost since, somehow. To visit Scotland was a great journey, for it was far more remote to the lads of our generation than is the case today. To see for example, No.60080 DICK TURPIN as I recall her in gleaming apple green, striding northwards with thirteen coaches of varnished teak, bearing the magic name "The Flying Scotsman" and carriage roofboards with the words "London-Edinburgh" and "London-Aberdeen", was to see something which remained in the memory ever after.

The A1s Nos.2558 TRACERY and 4478 HERMIT had worked on the Great Central main line just before the war in 1938/39 and in February 1949 nine were allocated there again, six to Leicester and three to Neasden. No longer were Pacifics allocated to Gorton, but the Leicester engines worked north as well as south. A large number of Southern Area A3s had a spell on the GC, the longest being Nos.60048, 60049, 60102, 60104, 60107 and 60111. The famous No.4472, (by now BR No.60103) FLYING SCOTSMAN went to

Leicester for a spell from June 1950 to November 1953 during which it did some fine work on the "South Yorkshireman" and "Master Cutler". Peter Townend remembers L.P. Parker commenting that that particular engine should return to the (GN) main line. It was good to see it running into King's Cross again on the up "Flying Scotsman" express, in the charge of the famous driver Bill Hoole, in the mid-1950s.

The A3s were slow to win approval on the GC Section since many of the older men favoured the engines that they had learnt their craft on, and the 4-4-0 and 4-6-0 types were the better starters. Once on the move the A3s and A1s could run fast, and the excellence of the GC permanent way encouraged drivers to give them their head, especially between Aylesbury and Nottingham where the gradients were favourable. It was only in 1957 when the line became the responsibility of the London Midland Region did they all return. The general impression of the A3s on the GC is that they were ran well despite difficult maintenance conditions at Leicester in the early 1950s. When they returned to the GN section they usually acquitted themselves well.

The Scottish Region of BR made trade union representations about the right-hand drive A1s and as a result in July 1950, four Pacifics were

Late in the life of steam, No.60080 DICK TURPIN passes Manors station, north of Newcastle, with a Glasgow relief. Manors station is sited on a sharp curve, and the driver of the Heaton A3 is no doubt taking matters carefully. The date is August 1st 1964; four months later the A3 was withdrawn. Boiler: 94A (27079) Tender: GN (5229) I.S. Carr.

exchanged. Nos.60090 GRAND PARADE, 60096 PAPYRUS, 60097 HUMORIST and 60098 SPION KOP were sent to Haymarket and Nos.60064 TAGALIE, 60065 KNIGHT OF THISTLE, 60066 MERRY HAMPTON and 60067 LADAS went south in exchange. Only No.60068 SIR VISTO of the original five remained in Scotland, and although the LMR classified Carlisle Canal shed as English, its allocation worked mainly to Scotland. I remember very well my amazement on seeing the 17.35 King's Cross-Newcastle, which was a Heaton turn as mentioned earlier, headed by No.60064 TAGALIE, with "Haymarket" on the buffer beam. No.60089 FELSTEAD followed north in February 1951 but alas no replacement was sent. No.60057 ORMONDE was a visitor running-in briefly but departed having raised youthful hopes. So while the Southern Area once had, briefly, the whole of the first batch of A3s, now it had none. The sole double chimney A3, No.60097 HUMORIST, was a particularly great loss and it was difficult to avoid the impression that despite some good running between Edinburgh and Newcastle, it would have been better appreciated on the GN Section.

One of the oddities of East Coast operation was that it was decided to provide two pilots at critical points. Darlington, having nothing bigger than B1s, received two A3s, Nos.60070 GLADIATEUR and 60076 GALOPIN. They were rarely seen in the south, and when they came up it was usually in place of a Top Shed A4 on the "Tees-Tyne Pullman". They were the only two A3s to survive in apple green so long after the rest that they outlived the BR blue livery and returned from overhaul in BR dark green. Obviously it had an effect on the mileages, as had the allocation to Carlisle on the engines there. York shed had no Gresley Pacifics post-war other than for a very short period when No.60074 was on loan, in contrast to the pre-war years. In fact the shed had very few main line diagrams on Anglo-Scottish express work.

It was interesting comparing the numbers of the various classes in operation. The new engines were already used on the principal trains, and when the Peppercorn A1s became more numerous the smaller wheeled Thompson Pacifics soon took a back seat. The A3s, as explained earlier, were classified 7P and were excluded from many of the main diagrams as a result. It was not, however, a happy time on the East Coast main line or the Motive Power Department, as failures mounted and failed locomotives had to be piloted in, or rescued from outstations such as Hitchin, Retford and Tweedmouth. Retford's small fleet of B1s became not infrequent visitors and the phrase 'Retford Pacific' gained a place in East Coast jargon.

So, in September 1951 we moved away from through working with engine changing being interposed once if not sometimes twice between London and Newcastle. Locomotives then had far less chance to overheat and regular manning could be revived. So enthusiasts went from an abundance of Tyneside visitors to a famine, and contrariwise, London engines were less often in Newcastle. This especially applied to the A3s and A4s from Tyneside. I remember the younger enthusiasts' great elation when a Tyneside visitor did pay a call. Nevertheless, the running of the A3s in the late 1940s and early 1950s was unspectacular at the southern end of the East Coast main line, and one had to admit that perhaps engine changing and the BR classification had some justification.

At Haymarket, the principle of allocating drivers to regular engines was introduced and spread through the main line links as far as was practicable. Whilst utilisation might have been marginally compromised, overall condition, availability and mileage accrual were steadily improved. The good condition of the locomotives is evident in the many illustrations in this book.

The principal expresses were mainly diagrammed for an 8P locomotive, which meant an A4 or Peppercorn A1. A3s only appeared when an 8P was unavailable. When a top link Grantham A1 was being washed out on a Wednesday night, we were usually treated to the magnificent sight of DONOVAN or one of her sisters on the fourteen coach "Aberdonian", roaring north. Likewise, at King's Cross, when top link A4s were stopped for examination, either a common user A4 or the shed's sole A3 No.60062 MINORU took their place. On an occasion when O.S. Nock was

No.60074 HARVESTER brings the empty stock for an up Liverpool express from Heaton carriage sidings into Newcastle Central. The A3 is now converted to left-hand drive, which with the earlier BR emblem, suggests the period 1953-57. The early stages of the Newcastle resignalling appear to be in hand from the new structures visible, putting the year at about 1955. V1 2-6-2T No.67642 is in the background in front of No.1 signal box, and a K1 2-6-0, 62043, heads a northbound freight. Boiler: 94A (27061) Tender: GN (5268) J.D. Smith.

An immaculate No.60068 SIR VISTO at York, four days after general overhaul at Doncaster Works, repainted in BR dark green but not yet converted to left-hand drive, August 16th 1952. Behind stands Peppercorn A1 No.60129 GUY MANNERING; it had originally been a York engine but had gone to Gateshead well before this shot was taken. Boiler: 94A (27005) Tender: A4 non-corridor (5637) J. Robertson, The Transport Treasury.

travelling south on the "Flying Scotsman", MALLARD had been stopped for repairs, and her regular driver, Alf Smith, had to use MINORU. As Ossie remarked, at Grantham the thin hissing exhaust of the Kylchap A1 was exchanged for the full-blooded roar of a Gresley Pacific on not the usual thirteen, but fourteen coaches. The A3s had a loud exhaust that became positively thunderous when working very hard as single blast engines. At the time, MINORU had a stiff regulator that would not move beyond two-thirds open, and her driver had to use a longer cut-off than usual. I saw her racing into London north of Finsbury Park, her smokebox door bearing testimony to the struggle farther north.

MINORU was Top Shed's sole A3 for a while and was a good runner. The top link men were given the A3 for shorter trips when their A4 was unavailable. I remember Ted Hailstone using her many a time when SILVER LINK was elsewhere, and running well with her. Then she was joined by a few more, especially for the summer timetable. The unofficially named "Bradford Flyer" was introduced in September 1952, and took a few years to become established. Britain did not rise so early in those days! It was a lighter train than usual, invariably worked by a Copley Hill A1 (Peppercorn) and tightly timed for the early 1950s. A Newcastle portion was added after a year or so, which created a new Doncaster duty to Newcastle and back. With a very short train indeed, there was some unusually fast running for that period and the Doncaster A3s

ran well. One of the Copley Hill top link, Driver Nicholls I believe, was an A3 enthusiast who believed in the use of a fully opened regulator. Every so often our morning run into London was enlivened by BLINK BONNY, SANSOVINO or BLAIR ATHOL thundering north at speed with their trainload of sleepy businessmen.

In the south, many of the old favourite visitors had been lost to the lineside youth, and while there is great satisfaction in seeing a well run railway with locomotives working their appointed services, there is a *frisson* in seeing a stranger in the camp. Our one Gateshead duty was dominated by Peppercorn A1s until late 1956. The salvation was that a number of Doncaster turns were used for running-in, principally the 19.10 lightweight parcels train to York, 102 down, which was worked by a Doncaster V2 as often as not. This turn was useful to run in express engines which had been repaired in the Works, and so it was compulsory viewing. The occasional sight of a gleaming Pacific heralded a rare visitor from Haymarket, Carlisle Canal or Neville Hill and sometimes even farther afield, with appropriate lineside celebrations. Often, disappointingly, it was one of our own. The sight of an ex-Works engine in immaculate fresh paintwork was always a sight for sore eyes.

Visits to Doncaster Works always excited the imagination over what visitors there would be there from the north, and we were rarely disappointed. It was fascinating to see familiar locomotives stripped down, to see what was in need of repair and how it was

done. The fact that a locomotive is a collection of many parts is brought home here. The repaired locomotive was reassembled and prior to painting it was not clear what its final identity would be. I remember younger members of the party visiting Doncaster Works practically performing cartwheels over the sight of the stripped down A3 which had the cabside number No.60086 GAINSBOROUGH, an engine almost unknown post-war in London. That is, until someone examined the frames and found that in fact it was No.60053 SANSOVINO, one of the Copley Hill trio!

In the late 1950s the Leeds District, which was divided between the E, NE and LM Regions of BR on operational use, was brought together under one of BR's periodical boundary adjustments. Holbeck and Wakefield sheds were re-designated 55 and 56 under the BR Depot numbering, and the ER Ardsley District (37) disappeared into Wakefield District. Later Neville Hill was added to Holbeck District. The effect of this minor piece of bureaucracy was in fact quite far reaching, since all of the Pacifics in the West Riding now came under one administration.

In 1954 Nos.60087 BLENHEIM and 60100 SPEARMINT of Haymarket had worked through to Leeds as an experiment, via the Waverley and Settle-Carlisle routes, but no more came of it, since the Scottish Region were not prepared to deal with the road learning and re-diagramming at Haymarket and Carlisle Canal. Now the A3s were deployed on the

No.60067 LADAS in the old platform 8 at King's Cross, while Peppercorn A1 No.60133 POMMERN is standing in platform 10. I would guess that POMMERN is on the 15.45 "West Riding" and LADAS is coupling on to the 15.50 to Leeds and York. The A1 was a Copley Hill stalwart, and the invariable choice for this turn in the summer of 1950. This photograph gives an interesting comparison between the A3 and the Peppercorn A1: the A1 was not quite an A3 with smoke deflectors. The longer smokebox and the different inclination of the outside steam pipes of the A1 can be seen clearly here. Boiler: 94A (27016) Tender: Non-corridor (5479) The Transport Treasury.

demanding Leeds-Carlisle route, and took to it with ease. The Royal Scots of Holbeck shed had worked with distinction, but the ride of the Pacifics was easier and superior. Now, crews found the fast and free steaming veterans very much to their liking, the easy riding of the A3s being the most attractive feature of all. It was good to hear crews' comments, and it was no surprise that the A3s should soon extend their operations to the old G&SW route into Glasgow. Initially the A3s were still single chimney engines, but they were altered to Kylchap double chimney soon after Doncaster started the conversions.

With the conversion of No.60055 WOOLWINDER to Kylchap double blast, the A3s were rejuvenated as the rest of the class followed suit. Once the crews realised how good the converted engines were, the A3s began to run as in their youth, with top speeds both more sustained and higher. Time was set back as the A3s took back the "Yorkshire Pullman" from King's Cross to Leeds from the A4s, and held it until April 1962 when the Deltic diesels took over. Top Shed cleaned their locomotives superbly and the sight of a gleaming A3 on the "Yorkshire Pullman" in the evening was something to savour. They worked turn and turn about with the Peppercorn A1s and A4s, and the crews appreciated the smoother riding of the Gresley engines. I remember one,

No.60109 HERMIT, then in her 36th year, running 73 consecutive return trips to Leeds on the "Yorkshire Pullman", filling in with night trips to Grantham as often as not. Grantham, initially not pleased at the loss of their prized Peppercorn A1s, took to the Kylchap A3s and made them run fast. They were quieter, which encouraged those who drove by the sound from the chimney to achieve greatly improved performances – one driver in particular!

No.60074 HARVESTER made annual visits to London, very unusually, to haul the International Harvester special train in the 1950s. No.60036 COLOMBO moved across Leeds to Copley Hill in 1961, but it was not until steam had to replace Type 4 diesels in 1961 did the other four Neville Hill A3s start to work south. It was with a feeling of utter astonishment that I realised the A3 in platform 5 at King's Cross on an overnight sleeping car train was not Top Shed's No.60066 MERRY HAMPTON but No.60086 GAINSBOROUGH. Sister A3s HARVESTER, SHOTOVER and TRIGO followed. Enquiries elicited the fact that the Neville Hill A3s were covering new diagrams intended for Type 4 diesels. They worked very intensive diagrams for some while in place of new Type 4 diesels, which had had a disastrous introduction. Starting from Leeds the A3 ran to

Newcastle on the down "Queen of Scots" Pullman then, after servicing, worked to King's Cross on a sleeping car express to astonish early morning commuters, and then returned to Leeds on the down "Queen of Scots" Pullman. They kept to this diagram for some while, the need for tube cleaning and "birds nesting"" at the tube ends being virtually eliminated by the stronger draught.

With the arrival of English Electric Type 4s, until some reliability had been achieved, the A3s and the other Pacifics had to work harder than in the old days. The 2,000HP diesels were more nuisance than benefit at first, and the Pacifics had to cope with deteriorating maintenance and diagrams of unprecedented intensity, planned for the diesels. A3s nearing the end of their fourth decade were expected to complete a journey and, within a few hours in which the locomotive was coaled, watered and oiled round and the fire cleaned, to be off on another long run. This was at a time when the Pacifics were running between London and Leeds or Newcastle, intermediate engine changing having been largely dropped. It was the arrival of the Deltics which sealed the fate of these remarkable locomotives, and with the introduction of Deltic diagrams in April 1962, followed by numbers of Brush (Class 47) Type 4s, steam had little time left. Steam was outlawed south of Peterborough, as BR sought to rid itself of "the old Adam" – and its heritage – and sell itself as a new, clean and efficient railway.

In Scotland however, pastures new beckoned, and Nos.60090 GRAND PARADE and 60094 COLORADO were sent to St. Rollox with twelve A4s. The Gresley Pacifics were put to work on the Glasgow-Aberdeen main line, and with even lighter loads they were fast runners. It was a pleasant surprise to catch a Glasgow express from Stirling and find that COLORADO was our locomotive. It was exhilarating as the A3, driven with a wide open regulator, accelerated rapidly to 60-70 mph from a standing start. But the steady withdrawal accelerated rapidly, until in early 1965 there were only three left in traffic. They were running their last few miles in Scotland between Edinburgh, Glasgow and Aberdeen. I managed to join a sleeping car train for Aberdeen very early in the morning at Dundee, hauled by Norman McKillop's old favourite, SPEARMINT. It was nostalgic to hear the A3 pull away, accelerating past the golf links, then pounding up to Carmont and out of Stonehaven. It was not a memorable performance but the sight and sound of the former star of non-stop running, with the familiar exhaust from her chimney, were things to savour.

When one looks at the work of the A3s and their life mileages, because they lived to a ripe old age in many cases, the figures are high. The highest was that of FLYING FOX, which must have almost reached 2.7m miles by the time she was withdrawn. Two years her junior, TRACERY was not far behind with over 2.5m miles, while Gateshead's ten A3s of 1924 all range from 2.1 to 2.3m miles. While Tyneside was thought to be slow to take to

Gresley's Pacifics, they certainly used them fully and maintained them well. Also one heard comments to the effect that North British built locos were not so good, but there was nothing wrong with the twenty A1s built in the second half of 1924. Detailed comments on statistical information are found in Chapter 5 and the *Appendices*.

For a large and long-lived design, the A3s had remarkably few bad accidents. It is freight engines which have to accept heavy shunts and insufficient braking distance as part of their lot, rather than express engines. As mentioned earlier, GRAND PARADE was damaged beyond repair in the Castlecary accident of December 10th, 1937, and a 28th A3 was built to replace her in 1938. MERRY HAMPTON was unusual in that it was twice derailed, both in Northumberland. The first occasion was deliberate, arising from strike action on May 10th 1926, though speed was very low; it was in a much more serious accident on October 26th 1947 when a driver ran through all warning signals and put most of his train "on the floor" as railwaymen describe it. In 1958 the bay platform at York was not long enough for the driver of COLOMBO to stop before his engine had mounted the buffer block and, I believe, destroyed a platform shop. NIGHT HAWK was damaged in one of the spectacular multiple collisions in which the Eastern Region of BR seemed to specialise in later years and was withdrawn as SOLARIO had been three years earlier.

The advent of diagrams for Ardsley and Copley Hill sheds to work the fast freights from and to Ardsley and Leeds brought, usually, V2s and sometimes B1s or even less into London, but the

down trains were sometimes used on Saturdays to return unbalanced engines to Leeds or Doncaster. The familiarity of the Yorkshire crews with the intricacies of GN signalling was not all that it should be at times. The GN was laid with sections of goods line to enable fast services to bypass slower ones, and such a line existed from Cadwell, north of Hitchin, to Arlesey where the four tracks became two over a level crossing. On a falling gradient it was all too easy to approach Arlesey too fast to stop should one either misread a clear down main aspect instead of the down goods, or simply not have a clear road. No less than three A3s over the years sailed down this section only to plunge into the soft swamp behind the down platform – CENTENARY, BLAIR ATHOL and ISINGLASS!

But the steam era was drawing to a close, and with it the good and bad things that went with it. Human nature is strange in that we seem able to remember in detail the things that we value, while ignoring the things that we do not. Many things improved with the departure of steam, but these are as nothing compared with the sights and memories of the machines of our youth. So it was a nostalgic occasion in 1964 when some of us travelled to Darlington, first behind the magnificent veteran FLYING FOX, as is described more fully in Chapter Five, and then the equally magnificent preserved FLYING SCOTSMAN. The railway scene was changing with the introduction of diesel and electric traction, but the sight and sound of a steam engine at speed was just as thrilling as it always was, even if it was rapidly becoming a thing of the past.

No.60040 CAMERONIAN, waiting on the west side at York station, with her crew sunning themselves on the adjacent track. The engine is just ex-Works, the only time Gateshead A3s looked clean in the early 1950s. The date must be May 1952, August 1953, or July 1955 as the engine is bearing the "Ferret and Dartboard". Boiler: 94A (27001, 35 or 77) Tender: GN (5253) The Transport Treasury.

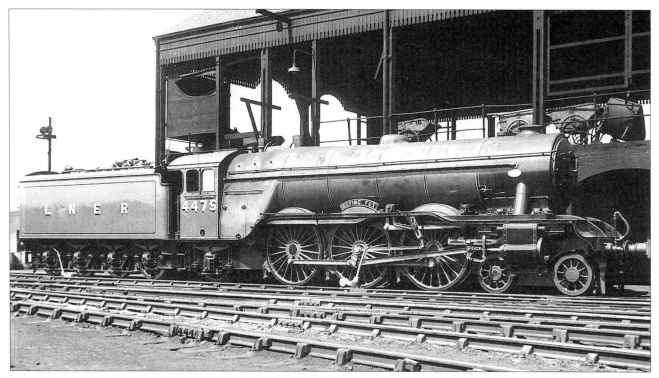

LNER No.4475 FLYING FOX was a regular on the "Non-stop" from the London end. She was coupled to a corridor tender for almost the whole time that A1s and A3s powered the train. With the prototype corridor tender attached she stands by the New England coaling plant. She has been overhauled and is running-in. Date June 16th 1935. Boiler 94(7878) Corridor tender (5323) L. Hanson.

BLINK BONNY at King's Cross station loco yard. The A1 has been fitted with long travel valves at its second general overhaul and is working from Grantham. The running number was carried on the tender and the cabside glass has yet to be fitted. The LNER livery, as with other pictures at the time, appears paler due to the film emulsion of the first half of the 20th century. I would put the date at the first half of 1928. Boiler:94 (original, 7768) Tender: GN (5260).

CHAPTER FOUR
DESIGN

It is now getting on for forty years since the last A3 Pacific ran in normal service on the nation's railway system, and one can look at the history of steam traction with a clearer perspective, unaffected by recent history. There are events in the story of the steam locomotive that are the defining moments, and the emergence of No.1470 was one of the very important ones. No.1470 was the second Pacific to be built, but whereas the Great Western's THE GREAT BEAR was too heavy for the Chief Civil Engineer and was therefore too confined in route availability to be successful, No.1470 was the first of a very long line of successful Pacifics and Green Arrows, nearly 400 locomotives. "Why did that young man have to build a Pacific?" G.J. Churchward is reported to have asked. "We could have had sold him ours!"

I have referred to the great advance that was achieved in the design of No.1470 – which it undoubtedly was – and no doubt the Directors of the Great Northern Railway were justly proud of the magnificent machine that Nigel Gresley had designed. But I think we often consider locomotive design and its history in its own narrow context without looking at the broader canvas of railway management, of which it is just a part. The events of nationalisation and privatisation, and the myriad reorganisations that have occurred between those times persuade us that other, perhaps more important issues were also on the minds of those who ran the Great Northern Railway.

The Grouping Act of 1922 meant that the GNR was to be part of the new London & North Eastern Railway, and for some while minds must have been concerned with what responsibilities and appointments awaited, and where they would be working after January 1st 1923. The six companies that were to form the new LNER were jockeying for position, for there were important jobs and responsibilities at stake. Careers could be advanced and the rewards increased! It was only to be expected. So the production of the GNR's first Pacific, as well as being Gresley's brilliant provision for a rapidly growing passenger business, was an expression of corporate virility by a company bidding for power in the new railway. The naming of the two locomotives after their company and their Chairman supports that view. The placing of an order for ten more locomotives not only strengthened the GNR position, but it had the inestimable benefit that the GNR would not have to find the investment itself!

It was a shrewd move which forced (as has been noted) a response from the North Eastern Railway, the largest and wealthiest partner of the six, in the shape of their two Pacifics late in 1922. Sir Vincent Raven was a celebrated engineer but Gresley, who became the Chief Mechanical Engineer of the LNER, was unlikely ever to have adopted Raven's drive on to the leading axle, with its relatively short connecting rods and three sets of Stephenson valve gear between the frames. Nevertheless, comparative trials were held and while the Gateshead crew of Driver Tom Blades and Fireman Fisher got some very good work out of No.2400, it was the Gresley locomotive that prevailed as having more potential for future development.

It is difficult to cast our minds back nearly eighty years. It seems to me that Gresley was working right up to the limit for coupled axle loading, and his A1 was built right up to the maximum overall size and weight allowed at the time. Henry Ivatt would have approved of the large boiler. It was based generally (as noted in Chapter Two) on that of the Pennsylvania Railroad's K4s Pacific, but Gresley preferred the round top firebox to the Belpaire used by the Pennsylvania. Although the Belpaire firebox allowed a greater evaporative surface area, especially round the firebox where it was of the maximum value, and a greater steam space, it was heavier, grate area for grate area, its construction and staying was more complex, and its subsequent maintenance was more costly. Gresley's large boilers were appreciably cheaper to maintain than the large Belpaire boilers of the LMSR Pacifics as demonstrated by the BR cost analysis in the 1950s. Maybe overall weight came into the reckoning as well. There was also the question of clearances and crew visibility that are particularly critical about the top corners of a large Belpaire firebox. This latter question was particularly relevant north of Newcastle, where there were tighter clearances

The 180 psi Pacific boiler was Doncaster's first taper boiler. It was strengthened to work at higher pressure with greater superheat for different successive designs but the essential design remained similar. It was not until 1941 that the next taper boiler design was produced, for the new light V4 2-6-2. Taper boilers are more complicated to roll and thus more expensive than parallel boilers, although the first cost of boilers cannot be compared works by works without taking works practice and the age of machinery into account. Remembering that the LNER was not a wealthy company, investment in new machinery for the workshops was unlikely to be a priority. The A1 boiler was allocated diagram No.94, and that boiler was a true and faithful servant for nearly 400 locomotives at 180, 220 and 250 psi. It gave little trouble, lasted well and, provided it was adequately draughted, met all demands for steam. It was used on all Pacifics, Green Arrows, Mikados and the rebuilt W1; the variations were allotted different diagram numbers but it was essentially the same boiler. The round top firebox, assisted post-war by the use of polyamide to prevent foaming and water carry-over, was perfectly satisfactory. With the conversion to A3, the 180 psi diagram 94 boilers were removed and either 94HP or 94A boilers fitted, the former with a dome and the latter a banjo dome. These circulated among the class, the stock being reinforced by the use of a number of diagram 107 A4 boilers in the 1950s and 1960s pressed to 220 psi. Outwardly these were identical with the 94A.

The A1 and A3 boilers gave little trouble in service. Gresley was a man with an open mind, and was always prepared to try something if he felt that it offered worthwhile improvement. In the 1930s different attempts were made to increase the exposure of steam to superheating, and hence raise its temperature, by modifying the superheater elements. Chapelon had used several more sophisticated designs, and Gresley decided to try Sinuflo elements on No.2746 FAIRWAY. The elements were shaped into a waveform to increase marginally the volume of the element, and hence steam temperature, for a given length. The modification in fact showed little advantage and was not pursued. A modification which did was the "Flat-Bridge" blastpipe, fitted as a trial in 1933. A feature of this design was the large chamber into which the cylinders exhausted, located between the valves and the standpipe itself. It softened the exhaust beats, reducing the sharp pull on the firebed at each exhaust beat. It was successful and the A1s and A3s were modified, and it became a feature of future large locomotive construction.

There is no doubt that the A1 and A3 frames, initially because of the

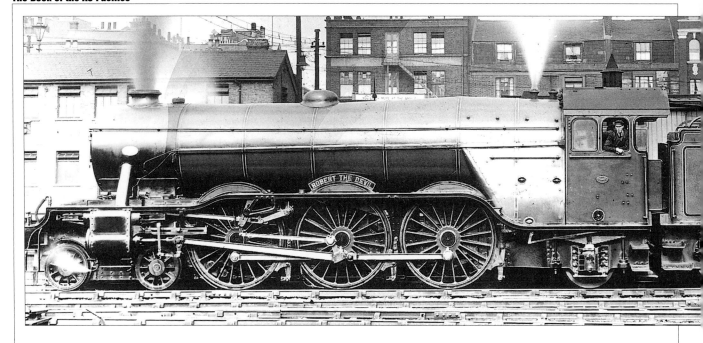

axleload limits, were less robust than was desirable. If Gresley had opted for higher pressure of the order of 220-225 psi in 1922, the weight of the boiler would have been that much heavier. A Pacific would have been impossible to build with as large as boiler as No.1470 at 220/225 psi within the Chief Engineer's 20 tons maximum axle loading, and Gresley would have had to settle for a smaller boiler with a lesser evaporative capacity. It was very difficult to estimate precisely the total weight of a design, comprising as it did a small number of very heavy components and a large number of essential and small parts. Locomotives, like most of us, also tend to get heavier with old age and modification and close control of a locomotive's weight, once the major components have been decided, is difficult. Of course it had to comply, but what was in fact working order had to be interpreted with some flexibility, if not imagination, at times. An inch less of water in the boiler would have reduced weight by about half a ton.

It always struck me that the assurance by the CME that his newest creation, when weighed in working order, has successfully complied with the limits laid down by the CCE, was one of the hardiest of railway myths. Of course, it was easy for the CCE, who simply set the limit; the CME had to abide by it. Some idea of the measures taken to remain within the law is given by some weights quoted in the RCTS Survey. The accepted weight of an A1 in working order was 92.45 tons but No.1470 weighed 92.7 tons, and No.4481 in 1926 was weighed at 97.5 tons. The excess was taken by the carrying axles, the bogie of No.4481 carrying 21.8 tons instead of 17.05, and the trailing axle carrying 18.5 tons instead of 15.4! In mitigation, the method of calculating underbridge strength was rudimentary and

locomotive weight would have had to be significantly in excess, for some while, before track maintenance costs were adversely affected.

Gresley's insistence on concentrated drive has not been widely discussed, although it was fundamental in his A1. It was also used later in France by André Chapelon for high power three cylinder locomotive types. Gresley disliked divided drive since he considered it would lead to accelerated wear on the flanges of the leading coupled wheels. Remember we are looking at 1922 when there were no transition curves, and in addition to any lateral control by the bogie, the leading coupled wheels had to absorb some of the lateral forces generated by running from straight to curved track and vice-versa. Certainly the technique of effective curve lubrication was not in use – if indeed it has come yet! Gresley's preferred method of lateral control was initially by the use of swing links, which require a good quality of maintenance and of permanent way. Where frequent and large lateral correcting control forces are needed, horizontal control springs are generally more positive and less affected by wear in the pivot points in a swing link system.

It had the advantage that the wheel balancing would have been carried out mainly on one axle. The disadvantage was of course the integrity of the driving crank axle, and the care with which it had to be assembled and maintained. With three cranks on that axle, the inside one being built-up, a high quality of workmanship was required in 1922 to produce a robust component to handle the power from three cylinders. Gresley admitted that his crank axle flexed in traffic, but *all* crank axles flexed to one extent or another. The alternative was divided drive, as used in many four cylinder engines, and was used later in the very successful

Peppercorn A1s. In theory, dividing the drive over two axles complicated the wheel balancing. In practice there was a slight deterioration in ride with divided drive especially when working hard, until the lateral control effected by the bogie control springs was corrected.

Concentrated drive enabled the use of conjugated gear more easily, as well as improvement of the layout of the cylinders, especially in relation to direct exhaust pipes. The conjugating levers were normally located ahead of the cylinders, but in the B17 and D49 designs they were behind. The unequal connecting rod lengths were hardly significant in practice. The need to place the middle cylinder on the locomotive's centreline, together with the compact layout of the cylinders under the blastpipe, initially limited the diameter of the piston valves to 8ins with 20in cylinders. In 1922 this was not a problem, but by the mid-1930s the importance of getting the piston valve diameter (and hence the cross sectional areas of the valves and ports) to at least half the diameter of the cylinders was beginning to be understood.

The conjugated valve gear has always been a bone of contention. Outside the LNER and at times within it, there was scepticism by many engineers. Why, one asks, since the advantages were set out in papers to the Institution of Locomotive Engineers by both Holcroft and Spencer? Outside the UK some 400 three cylinder locomotives were so fitted, including the 88 Union Pacific 4-12-2s. The conjugated valve gear was a great benefit and enabled Gresley to build his Pacific. It took some time to finalise its development, but it eliminated a great deal of valve mechanism between the frames, and simplified the driver's preparation work. It also saved the extra weight of

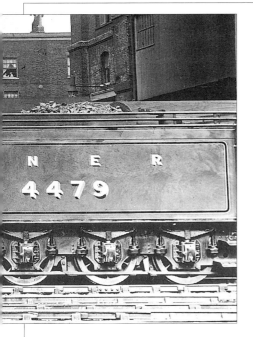

a third independent valve gear, important in 1922. Gresley's Pacific was five tons lighter than Raven's. Overall, the Gresley three cylinder layout, with concentrated drive and conjugated valve gear, was a compact and very effective design. Only when his successors attempted to modify the design did they realise just how neat an arrangement it was.

The disadvantages of the 2:1 gear itself were few but important. Valve gear performance was critical as the 1925 Exchanges confirmed and no doubt many engineers would not have been happy with a system in which any wear or maladjustment to the outside gears would immediately reflect double that amount on the operation of the third cylinder. During the war years and after, the Gresley engines suffered along with all other engines, and the effects of wear and maladjustment in the axleboxes, frames and valve gear were plainly audible with the three cylinder engines. In my early years there were some terrible noises to be heard from run-down A3s and V2s. The running gear certainly had to be kept in good order and when during wartime it could not, one could understand Thompson's concern. If not properly cleaned and lubricated, the bearings wore.

In the early days the large 2:1 conjugating lever was not so firmly held, but stronger frame supports were designed and made. The gear was often blamed for failures, quite wrongly, since the real weakness was the design of bearing used at Doncaster. It was shown with No.2751 HUMORIST that it caused unequal power outputs from the three cylinders, and it was easy to extrapolate from there to an overworked and therefore overheated middle big end. The equal sharing of power between the back and forward strokes of three cylinders, rather like

perpetual motion, remains a concept much to be desired but unattainable in reality. For example in the GWR 'King' 4-6-0 tests, a variation of 18% was shown between the power output of two adjacent cylinders on each side. (S.O. Ell, 1933). The 2:1 gear, in good order, did not cause a major inequality between the strokes of the three cylinders that could not have existed with a three cylinder engine with three independent sets of valve gear. Good lubrication was critical. Certainly the A3s, and the A4s, had middle big end failures, often very public ones, and no doubt any increase in power output coupled with the relative lack of cooling by the slipstream had been more than the bearing could stand.

Perhaps the use of Walschaerts valve gear allied to Lentz oscillating cam poppet valves as in the Chapelon rebuilds in France would have improved steam flow but the problem of actuating the middle cylinder valve remained. Certainly the setting of the piston valves required experience and skill, and the setting for the inside piston valve required compensation for the effect of expansion by the outside piston valves where the mechanism lay ahead of the cylinders. Of course there was the danger that lubrication of the inside connecting rod ends, big and little, might be overlooked. The big ends were the most important bearings on the locomotive.

In 1922, special cast iron and steel with the requisite qualities of resilience and hardness were very much in their infancy. Piston rings for steam locomotives were of heavier and of broader section initially. The change in 1926 to narrow piston rings enabled a much better seal to be made against steam leakage. Three narrow rings would have flexed more closely to the cylinder wall profile or valve bore than the broad rings that were many times less flexible. The dramatic reduction in steam leakage and greater economy in working experienced in the late 1920s on the LNER was a repetition of what had been found elsewhere.

Looking back with more than half a century of hindsight, it is puzzling that a device or technique that succeeded in a design was not copied back into earlier designs. The discovery of the advantages of a Kylchap exhaust in MALLARD did not rouse the LNER to modify 78 of the 79 A1s and A3s for example, something which had to wait for another twenty years and 300,000 extra tons of coal to pass by. In its restoration, the work carried out on FLYING SCOTSMAN is of interest.

The use of an A4 diagram 107 boiler has allowed the use of a working boiler pressure of 250 psi, as it was designed for. Allied to this the 19in cylinders were bored out to 19¾ins at first, giving a nominal tractive effort in excess of 40,000lb. More recently a new 19in liner has been inserted bringing the locomotive into line with Doncaster practice. She retains the Kylchap double blastpipe, which ensures that the engine steams freely with lower grade coal. Performance at high speed, however, in theory would be limited at high rates of steaming by the relatively small 8in piston valves, although that is not a problem in preservation.

During restoration, two changes have been made which were long overdue. The main steam pipe emerged from the smokebox vertically and turned through right angle bends between the superheater header and the outside cylinders, and it did not follow closely the characteristic shape of the cladding at all. The overhauled engine was fitted with more direct pipes to ease the steam flow without affecting its appearance. Also the diameter of the main steam pipe is 7in as in the 94A boilers fitted to the last batch of A3s and to the A4s, but in the A3s this was throttled down to 5ins at the header originally. Was the change from five to seven inches tracked through the design to ensure that it was not negated beyond the regulator? The original cast iron headers fractured and were replaced by cast steel versions. A superheater header was a complex and expensive casting, and was only replaced when necessary, especially taking the cost of modifying flanges into account.

But when we have finished discussing and examining the technical aspects, we should also pause to consider the appearance of No.1470 and her sisters, for that is what engages the minds of many who enjoy railways without a thought for technicality. Gresley's first Pacific had a simplicity of line, as had its predecessors by Gresley and Ivatt before him. The familiar Doncaster smokebox door, the "face" of a locomotive, was reassuring, the great sweep of huge coupled wheels with the neat, perfectly proportioned valve gear, the cab, just right, and the enormous taper boiler, again perfectly in proportion to the rest of the locomotive. Gresley and his design team at Doncaster were not merely good engineers: they were artists too, in creating a machine of balance and proportion. Alter the pitch of the boiler, the chimney, the cab, move the bogie, re-space the coupled wheels, and so on, and the effect would be spoilt. It is an engineering truism that "if it looks right, then it is right", and No.1470 bore that out in 1922.

The moment every photographer dreams of! DONOVAN, still as an A1, on an up express north of a very rural Potters Bar, meets HUMORIST on a down express. Both Pacifics are spotlessly clean. The shot is doubly interesting since HUMORIST ran as a conventional A3 from 1929 to 1932 and possibly from 1933 to 1937 as well. It is not clear that the A3 has a cabside glass screen and if not the earlier period would be right; otherwise the date is indeterminate. The rest of the time the loco was either subject to a number of experimental smoke deflection arrangements, or had a double chimney. Boiler: 94 (No.2546) 94HP (No.2751), both numbers unknown. Tender: GN (5256 and 5265 respectively) G. Goslin, The Gresley Society.

CHAPTER FIVE
PERFORMANCE AND POWER

The A1s and A3s could run very fast, and smoothly. In the preparatory testing prior to the introduction of the "Silver Jubilee" and the A4 in 1934, No.4472 FLYING SCOTSMAN topped Stoke Bank at 81 mph with a lightweight train of 147 tons gross, en route for Leeds. On the up run from Leeds to Kings Cross, now with 207 tons, the A1 was opened out approaching Grantham, and reached 100mph for the first authenticated occasion, down Stoke bank. In early 1935 No.2750 PAPYRUS worked a similar test train to Newcastle, 217 tons gross. The climax of 536.6 miles of high speed running was the descent of Stoke bank, where, between Little Bytham and Essendine, the A3 reached a maximum of 108mph, a record for a conventional unstreamlined steam locomotive. Nor was that the end of fast running, for the run continued to achieve a record time for the Peterborough-King's Cross section. Both achievements were authenticated by dynamometer car records. Whilst the loads were relatively small, the high power output was absorbed in

acceleration to the high peak speeds and in the increased wind and frictional resistances at high speed.

For a locomotive that astonished everybody at its size when it was first showed to the public, the Gresley non-streamlined Pacific, surprisingly, does not figure among those locomotives that achieved exceptional feats of power. Until 1935, the cylinder horsepower required to haul 500 tons averaging 60 mph from Tallington to Stoke, or run at 80 mph on the level, as the A1s and A3s did habitually, was as high as any in the country. But they had little cause to attempt short bursts of very high power. I suppose the East Coast main line, lacking the equivalent of a Shap, Beattock, Ais Gill or Blea Moor, requires less in the way of steam spectaculars on heavy gradients. The A3s, to give them their later description, on their home ground could pull and run fast economically. So, with good track, why make hard work for one's mate and the locomotive? One looks in vain, however, for any huge power outputs of the category achieved later by more modern and bigger

designs. What Gresley had aimed for was a powerful locomotive by 1920s standards, but economical and reliable too. That he did, handsomely, and the quality of their work on heavy loads at high speed was outstanding. The A3 with a single chimney would, I suppose, develop a peak of around 1700-1800IHP at a speed of 50-80mph. When they were fitted with a Kylchap double blastpipe, that figure increased to over 2,200IHP. An exceptional effort might exceed those values marginally for very short periods.

The Kylchap blastpipe was deceptive for drivers who worked their locomotives according to the sound of the exhaust and the draught. Ben Glasgow was not the last of the heavy-handed drivers. The quieter exhaust at first led to over-firing, only a thin fire being necessary with a Kylchap. Where a few drivers, despite all that had been said and done, used longer cut-offs with a partially closed regulator, the Kylchap engines could certainly burn coal. It was by comparison with the simple blastpipe and chimney casting a more

It was normal practice at King's Cross, in busy periods, for Belle Isle (of immortal memory) to despatch two locos from the loco spur over the up independent into the terminus rather than send them separately. The up independent and down main one occupied the central bore of Gasworks Tunnel. Pacifics were not allowed to run in tandem on the GN main line due to weight restrictions at Digswell viaduct at Welwyn, the Ouse underbridge at Huntingdon, and the Dyke underbridge at Newark. Whether they should have been so restricted is an entirely different question, of course. People neither familiar with

the East Coast main line nor aware of this practice assumed that double headed Pacifics were an occasional sight on the East Coast main line. I would guess that this is the evening rush, and ISINGLASS had backed on to her train in old platform 8. The unidentified A4 would then couple off and shunt to her train, probably in old platform 10. The date is August 5th 1955. The boiler is a 1930 one, originally No.8225, still going 25 years later and a good example of the longevity of Doncaster boilers. Boiler: 94HP (27037) Tender: GN (5231) B.K.B. Green, Initial Photographics.

TRACERY, the A3 with the second highest mileage, was an old friend that was always around somewhere on the GN. Well cleaned, she is pulling away from old platform 7 at King's Cross. It is a good study of the handsome A3, even with a double chimney. The date is not given but must be after July 1958: I would plump for 1959. Boiler: 94A (27075) Tender: GN (5284) N. Lester, The Transport Treasury.

complicated device. However, the much stronger and more even draught across the tube bank reduced ash deposits in the tubes and at the tube ends, greatly reducing the need for tube cleaning, contrary to the view held at the BTC and elsewhere on BR. For those who adjusted their driving methods to the quieter exhaust and ran with a thin fire, the modified locomotives were extremely economical, and a Kylchap A3 would run into King's Cross with a surprisingly huge pile of coal still in the tender. Tests had shown that the Kylchap engines showed an economy of 6-7% compared with a single chimney engine.

The performances of the A1s and A3s have been fully documented by Cecil J. Allen and O.S. Nock in the "Railway Magazine" under "Locomotive Practice and Performance", and the huge volume of performance data cannot be adequately summarised here. One can go back to No.1471's run in 1922, hauling a 610 ton train to Grantham in 122 minutes and later worthy efforts, but it is the high speed runs which naturally take the eye. In 1931, No.2547 DONCASTER brought a 235 ton train up from Peterborough to London in 66mins 10secs, 62mins net, and six days later No.2743

FELSTEAD brought the "Breakfast Flyer", up from Grantham in 92mins 42secs, 89½mins net, loaded to 310 tons. With 92mph at Barnet and 75 at Holloway North, Driver Watson was anticipating conditions at least fifty years later! Then came the two high speed runs by No.4472 and No.2750 mentioned earlier.

With the arrival of the A4s, the A3s were somewhat overshadowed, but good work continued. No.2503 FIRDAUSSI of Gateshead was used successfully on the "Silver Jubilee" to assess what reserve the A3s had in running the train. There was the famous run in 1936 on the down "Scarborough Flyer" by A1 Pacific No.4473 SOLARIO driven by Driver Joe Duddington of MALLARD fame, delayed at Welwyn Garden City. The 180 psi A1 recouped the arrears by keeping to the passing times from Hitchin to Selby that were set for the running of the "Coronation" the following year. Joe Duddington may have interpreted his speed limits rather more liberally than usual to keep up speed but for all that it was a superb run. Remarkably, this was with 395 tons instead of 325, fortuitously with a clear road, averaging just under 80 mph from Grantham to Doncaster. That the A1 could handle the timing

was demonstrated again two years later, this time with the "Coronation" itself.

The magnificent 1936 run was eclipsed by an even more startling achievement by the same A1 when on May 17th and 18th 1938. On the "Coronation" she relieved A4 No.2512 SILVER FOX which had failed with a hot middle big end at Grantham. Onwards the run was plagued with three Temporary Speed Restrictions ('TSR's) and arrival was 55 minutes late. As luck would have it, No.4473 was the one engine that had been fitted with an experimental steam-operated scoop in 1929, and it was still fitted in 1938. The Haymarket men were unfamiliar with it and unable to use it at Lucker, so had to take water at Newcastle and Berwick. For some reason not apparent even now, it seems that No.4473 was returned the following day right through to London. It is hard to imagine that Haymarket had no A4 available for the "Coronation" of all duties, and could not borrow one from Gateshead either. Even an A3 would have that edge in speed on the level and uphill. But SOLARIO remarkably kept to the running time, arriving 16 late despite four TSRs and taking water during the brief Newcastle stop, which would account for all the arrears and more. It was a remarkable achievement for a 180 psi A1 to work the "Coronation" right through from Edinburgh to London, presumably with the 325 tons summer loading, and net of all delays gaining say five minutes on the six hour schedule then in force. No.4473, according to "Yeadon's Register" (Irwell Press, 1990, now Book Law Publications) had been 11 months out of shops, must certainly have been on the high side of 50,000 miles, and was coupled to a GN type tender. It must have called for a very high standard of enginemanship on the part of the crews especially Driver Auger and his fireman of King's Cross, who brought the A1 from Newcastle.

On March 22nd 1939 No.4491 gave way to No.2595 TRIGO, with a hot axlebox, and Driver Nash of King's Cross made a remarkable run to London with the A3 to arrive right time, despite several delays, in 225 mins net. Remarkably, the Haymarket driver (whose name is fortunately not known) also ran No.4493 hot at Tweedmouth *two days later*, and the penultimate A3 No.2507 SINGAPORE, again in the hands of Driver Nash, took over at Newcastle. After delays there (arising from the fireman overlooking the need to couple the locomotive as well as the train heating pipe) No.2507 regained nine minutes of the arrears as well as those occurring en route. In both cases the uphill work must have been magnificent, and as the A3 in each case

was not fitted with a Flaman speed recorder the maximum down Stoke Bank was most likely well into three figures for some distance. No.2507's time to London with 290 tons winter loading was 222½ mins net, an average of 72.4mph start to stop, a record for the A3s. What Driver Nash said to his fireman at Newcastle has fortunately also not been recorded for posterity, but presumably that worthy paid for his oversight with a wet shirt. SINGAPORE was one of the A3s fitted with a larger main steam pipe and was still carrying the original boiler at the time.

Focussing on the high speed exploits of the A3s is to look at one aspect of their work, and it was their performance at speed with heavy loads, referred to earlier, that commands admiration. Details can be found for example in the "Railway Magazines" of 1933 and 1938. No.2503 FIRDAUSSI hauling 570 tons, averaged 59 mph from Tallington to Stoke, 15.3 miles, a superb effort. The famous No.4472 FLYING SCOTSMAN when an A1, with her regular driver, the equally famous Bill Sparshatt, worked 615 tons from Grantham to King's Cross in just under 110 mins running time with a stop at Peterborough. The Haymarket A3 No.2796 SPEARMINT on the up "Flying Scotsman" made up to 540 tons, reached and held 44mph up to Stoke summit from the Grantham start, after which she accelerated this

heavy train up to 90mph by Essendine, and held 75-76 on the level before Sandy. The 105.45 miles to London were run in 104mins 45secs, or 102½ mins net with this heavy load. In the reverse direction No.2744 GRAND PARADE passed Peterborough in just under 74 mins with a train of 530 tons. Farther north the opportunity for fast running was generally much less with the numbers of heavy freights and speed restrictions for colliery area workings.

During the war, with speeds very much lower, some huge loads were hauled. The wartime timetable reduced the number of expresses, understandably, to allow for reduced manpower and the need to run freight. As a consequence, train loads had increased to unprecedented levels by Easter 1940. A famous exploit at the time was that of No.2549 PERSIMMON; still an A1, it worked one of the heaviest trains, 850 tons, from Peterborough to King's Cross losing only 2mins on the 93 minute schedule then in force. During the war years loads continued at high levels, still in the 600-700 tons range, even after some services were restored. The schedules were of course undemanding in terms of speed but delays were frequent and sometimes lengthy. In the post-war years it became clear that the A3s were not as dominant as before 1939, something which has been mentioned earlier. There were some 90 newer engines, most fitted with double

WOOLWINDER, waiting at York to take over an up express. As the A3 was fitted with the small deflectors in October 1959 at general overhaul, and she seems to have become quite travel stained since, the date seems like summer 1960. There were a number of turns worked by King's Cross from York especially on summer Saturdays, the up "Norseman", the "Scarborough Flyer", and the 11.00 from Edinburgh and its reliefs. A popular engine, WOOLWINDER was one of the early withdrawals in 1961. Boiler: 107 (29301) Tender: GN (5286) The Transport Treasury.

No.60066 MERRY HAMPTON on an up express, probably the 9.50 from Leeds, overtaking an inner suburban train formed of the unforgettable Quad-Art sets, on September 10th 1960. The A3 is not up to the usual Top Shed standard, if she worked the down "Yorkshire Pullman" the evening before, but she was only three months from having had a general overhaul and cannot have been too bad! The cab with the high ventilator, originally on ST. SIMON, can be seen clearly here. Boiler: 107 (29279) Tender: GN (5223) D.M. Alexander, The Transport Treasury.

blastpipes, and steaming was not a problem for them. Although the various test trains run post-war featured good work, sometimes outstandingly good, the A3s gave the impression of not always being as free steamers, post-war, as the newer locomotives.

My earliest memories of the East Coast route were of the A3s as the élite, filthy as often as not but identified by names, with those great coupled wheels rolling round and their impressive exhaust. Then of course, as war ceased and things started to return to normal, there was the joy of seeing old favourites in apple green livery. So it was something of a shock when I rode behind the aristocracy of the former LNER, for the running was not very good. Certainly there were Temporary Speed Restrictions in abundance from wartime arrears, delays were legion due to freights of all sorts crawling over the layouts, schedules had expanded and fuel was not good. But the operation seemed to symbolise the country; uninspired, apathetic and drained after its wartime efforts.

It was interesting, for example, to compare the steaming of No.2746 FAIRWAY on test fitted with experimental superheater elements, before the war with its work after 1945. The pre-war run showed that the boiler pressure, despite the locomotive being worked hard, had been maintained

between 200 and 220 psi for most of the run, up hill and down dale. Experiences after the war did not have the same energy and reliability, and all too often one gave up recording a thoroughly dismal performance. Now and again there was some good running, but it was not the rule. When on test, the running was good but this was not regularly reflected in daily performance so often. Crews were unwilling to work engines hard when newer free-steaming alternatives were available.

In an exercise to verify the standard sectional times calculated for various increments of train weight, a high mileage A3 was selected as the motive power and some very good work was performed by No.60056 CENTENARY on test trains. It showed that the locomotives were still capable of hard running but only if the drivers and, by implication, the fireman, were prepared to work the locomotive harder. Understandably, normally they were not. Some were quite adamant that they would not press overmuch to recover time lost by others.

The new timetable of October 1956 introduced more trains, with tighter scheduled and the loadings reduced. I am sure that railway history does not give enough credit to Gerry Fiennes, the Line Traffic Manager, for the rebuilding of the East Coast main line timetable, which created the opportunity for the

older Pacifics to play their part. I had a good example of their work on lighter loads in summer 1957 when the "Morning Talisman" was introduced. No.60108 GAY CRUSADER had eight coaches, roller bearing, and the locomotive was fitted with self-cleaning screens. This imparted a strange exhaust to the engine, something like a three cylinder WD 2-8-0 and quite unlike the normal A3 sound. Driver Gymer was not afraid to use full regulator on this light load, and as the conversion to continuous welded rail was in full swing, there were many TSRs and consequent delays. The A3 roared up to the high eighties time and time again, and reached 96mph near Arlesey. The 34 year old Pacific was riding smoothly and the driver had no hesitation in letting the locomotive go. It was a joy to savour, and a revelation that the veterans could still run fast.

What really gave the A3s a new lease of life was conversion to double Kylchap exhaust, as has been emphasised earlier. As it happened, the BTC was unaware that the change had been made, and there is no doubt that, if it had known, the Commission would have opposed it. Fortunately it was too late, and magazine articles devoted to locomotive performance included many fine runs by double chimney A3s. Their common feature was that drivers, now confident that their firemen could easily supply all the steam they required, were prepared to run fast. I will quote just one example. Newly returned from Doncaster Works in 1959, Gateshead's No.60075 ST. FRUSQUIN took over the down "Flying Scotsman" at Newcastle from diesel No.D208, delayed further south and now 24mins late. By 1959 the 10.00 had been reduced to 420 tons. With this load, 60075 halved the arrears by whirling the train past Berwick, 66.1 miles in 60½mins, and by Dunbar she was only 7 mins late. The time from Newcastle to Edinburgh was 113mins, 72.5mph start to stop, a record for an A3. The average from Berwick to Dunbar, over Penmanshiel summit, was 69.2mph, and the speed descending past Belford was probably rather higher than the limits permitted.

One of the last runs that I had with an A3 was the Gresley Society excursion to Darlington on May 2nd 1964 referred to in the previous chapter. It was hauled from King's Cross to Doncaster and back by No.60106 FLYING FOX. The Doncaster-Darlington leg was behind No.4472 FLYING SCOTSMAN. I travelled on the locomotive from King's Cross to Peterborough with Chief Inspector George Harland. Our driver was a well-known friend from No.2 link, Sid Piggin: the fireman had signed on confident of an easy day on a diesel locomotive, and found to his dismay that he was wrong. Nevertheless he fired No.60106 admirably and she ran well to Doncaster. The safety valves lifted at 205 psi, a little light, but the steam

pressure was kept well up to maximum. We had only a light train of 325 tons gross, and we reached Peterborough in just over 71 mins. For much of the journey the driver was working the A3 with full regulator and 15% cut-off, and on the fast section from Hitchin to Huntingdon was covered at an average of 84.4 mph with a brief maximum of 95mph.

On the return run I reminded George that we were now permitted to run at 100 mph from Stoke to Tallington quite legally, but his reply was a gruff reminder that this locomotive was 41 years old. My rejoinder was to remind him that if the engine was unsafe at 100 mph, it was hardly much safer at 90mph, and we had already done 95mph on the down run. We had a Doncaster crew now, and the pressure varied initially since the fireman had acclimatised to diesel traction. We ran well and on the approach to Stoke with the needle of the boiler pressure gauge on the red mark, No.60106 was going well at 70-75 mph. Once again, and for the last time, one felt the level of vibration and noise in the cab increase as we climbed up from the Trent Valley. Once clear of Stoke Tunnel Driver Green turned to George Harland and said "Well? What do you want?" The latter thought, checked the riding, and said "Let her go".

At full regulator at 15% FLYING FOX accelerated away downhill, speed rising rapidly. Now the noise level changed slightly as the speed rose after Stoke and the motion of the engine quietened. The exhaust lay in a grey streak over the boiler and cab, and

all the sensations of a Gresley Pacific at high speed could be felt for the last time. We hit a low joint near Little Bytham at 90mph causing at least one person on the footplate to think his last moments had come. The speedometer needle gradually rose until for 5-6 miles the needle was on 100 mph, although the speed was actually less, before the Driver saw that Essendine's distant was on and braked hard. It was an unforgettable moment as the old engine made one more sprint before she was finished.

So, in happier days at least for railways, we would see, coming towards us on the East Coast main line, a long train of teak coaches with a familiar shaped apple green locomotive at the head. The exhaust would be growing, and we could see the white steam drifting from the safety valves. The fireman would be building up his fire at the back, the driver would have the regulator wide open, the locomotive well linked up, and be scanning the road ahead for his signals. As he passes, the exhaust note changes, and there is the name – FLYING FOX, SOLARIO, GLADIATEUR, NIGHT HAWK or WINDSOR LAD, above the circling motion, and there are the great wheels loping along. Then she is past, exhaust barking away, the great green tender sliding past, and then the teak carriages with their passengers, and finally the flickering red tail lamp. We would probably watch the A3 into the distance, the exhaust growing fainter and the smoke dispersing. Now that is what an express really looked like!

The restoration of the "Queen of Scots" Pullman after the 1939-45 war came on July 5th 1948; this is the train starting out of the old platform 10 at King's Cross behind an immaculate apple green ROYAL LANCER. She is bearing the old plate headboard that was later replaced in cast duralumin as with all headboards. Boiler: 94A (9515) Tender: GN (5267) G. Goslin, The Gresley Society.

No.60054 PRINCE OF WALES, in an external condition that Grantham would once have disowned, rolls into old platform 8 at King's Cross, probably with a Newcastle express. Some idea of the tortuous layout can be gained from this shot. On the left beyond the clearance bar in platform 10 is a tandem (one lead, or set of points, inside another). It was this connection, or something very similar, that Driver Sparshatt struck with No.4472 FLYING SCOTSMAN at excessive speed on his record run of November 30th 1934, leaving wheel flange marks on the railhead! The Transport Treasury.

SOLARIO, just transferred from Doncaster to Gorton, at Nottingham Victoria with the 14.15 Manchester London Road to Marylebone, May 1939. The A1s left the GC during the war, but returned afterwards, then as A3s, in greater numbers. Boiler: 94 (7700) Tender: GN (5254).

An immaculate No.60044 MELTON races past Greenwood signalbox on July 8th 1953. The train is almost certainly the 9.15 from York, a Doncaster turn that MELTON was used on very often, returning with the 15.50 to Leeds and Bradford. Her exceptional condition was due to her use as either on the Royal train or as a standby. Many of us will shed a silent tear for Greenwood, a box which probably had more illegal visits than any other, and was the subject of a famous Terence Cuneo painting. Boiler: 94A (27033) Tender: GN (5274) B.K.B. Green, Initial Photographics.

It is evening at King's Cross, and LNER No.56 CENTENARY is about to leave with an express, probably the 17.30 to Newcastle. The date quoted is September 9th 1948, but I suspect it should be 1947, just after CENTENARY was restored to apple green livery. The Railway Executive would have had heads on plates if they thought that one of their engines was still bearing the prohibited initials a year later! G. Goslin, The Gresley Society.

What boys of all ages spent hours gazing at – the cab of a steam engine. KNIGHT OF (the) THISTLE at New England in 1963/4. The cab has been altered very little over nearly forty years, but the vertical handrail has been lengthened and the cut-out behind the driver was reduced when bucket seats were fitted, to reduce slipstream draught. The firebox has the typical handholes of the 94A boiler for washing out and examination, including the odd one in the cab sidesheet. On the cab side is the glass sidescreen added from 1929 onwards to protect the driver as he watched the line ahead, to read his signals. In the cab one can see the main brake valve with the operating handle down out of sight, 'on'. The small handle visible is the blower valve, used to force a draught up the chimney. This would stimulate the fire on the grate when the engine had been lit up from cold and had made a little steam. It was also used to draught the fire when coasting, or running into a tunnel when there was a danger of a 'blowback'. High up in the cab above the firebox is the manifold with steam supplied to the various gauges and the slacker pipe. Under the running board one can see the cables from the AWS receiver. It is a good view of the Cortazzi axlebox in its shaped guides or horns at the rear of the frame, although how it continued to function with so much dirt and dust I cannot imagine. The tender and Cortazzi springs can be seen, held by hangers and secured under large washer blocks. These were adjusted when the locomotive was weighed, to take more or less weight in order to comply with the maximum axle weights allowed. Boiler: 94A(27062) Tender: GN (5285) The Transport Treasury.

CHAPTER SIX
THE LOCOMOTIVES; SOURCES, STATISTICS AND APPEARANCES

SOURCES

There is a wealth of information published about all the Gresley Pacifics. My introduction was "The Gresley Pacifics of the LNER" by Cecil J. Allen, which was compulsory reading. Well written, it was however numerically inaccurate by later standards. Later I came by a copy of O.S. Nock's "Locomotives of the LNER". Then there were successive works by F.A.S. Brown and others, from which one learnt more of the story. The first detailed history was by the Railway and Correspondence Society which published an exhaustive account entitled "The Locomotives of the LNER" commencing in 1963 with the preliminary survey, and ten years later part 2A dealing with the Pacifics of all types was published. This contained an enormous amount of information about both the classes and individual locomotives, and has no doubt fathered many articles since. Much of the information given in this account has appeared before in the RCTS Survey.

In the view of the author, the three important definitive works on this subject are, firstly, the RCTS part work, "Locomotives of the LNER" mentioned above, although this needs to be read in conjunction with two later works. The second is W.B. Yeadon's "Yeadon's Register of LNER Locomotives", the first volume of which deals with the A1s and A3s. These volumes give building and repair dates for each locomotive, modifications, tenders coupled, liveries, and allocation. It is an incredible monument to the dedication of one who was not even a railwayman, but a devout enthusiast. The whole astounding amount of detail is well illustrated.

The third is my friend Peter Townend's definitive work "East Coast Pacifics at Work". Peter Townend, as many will know, started his career in Doncaster Plant alongside many of these Pacifics, and became Shedmaster at King's Cross. A great deal of further detail is given by a man who knew the engines inside out, and who was principally responsible for the Indian Summer of the Pacifics on the East Coast route. There are other publications which offer various details but these are the three principal and authoritative ones. For any person researching this subject, a study of these three volumes are a *sine qua non*.

In addition to these sources, there is an enormous amount of recorded information on performance, described by Cecil J. Allen, O.S. Nock and Norman Harvey, chiefly in the "Railway Magazine's" long running "Locomotive Practice and Performance" series of articles, but also in "Trains Illustrated" and the "Railway World".

APPENDICES

I have set out the important features of the locomotives' history in Appendix A. This is intended to define the important dates but not to cover the minutiae of their detailed history. The Appendix gives the principal dates for the locomotives' building, rebuilding and withdrawal. Details not included can be found in the appropriate parts of the RCTS Survey or "Yeadon's Register". The locomotives underwent a number of changes in their long careers that are recorded on individual record cards which survived up to 1953 when the standard British Railways Engine Record Card was introduced. These survive at the Public Records Office at Kew. The information they contained was first published by Irwell Press in the "Yeadon's Registers" which are still in print with Book Law Publications and there is no point in duplicating the information here. So in the absence of Works details, allocations, boiler changes and so on this "Book of the A3 Pacifics" represents something of a departure from most Irwell Press "Books Of..."

No.60093 CORONACH on Haymarket shed turntable, June 28th 1952. The Carlisle A3 has only been back from general overhaul a month, hence her good condition. Boiler: 94A(27004) Tender: GN (5287) J. Robertson, The Transport Treasury.

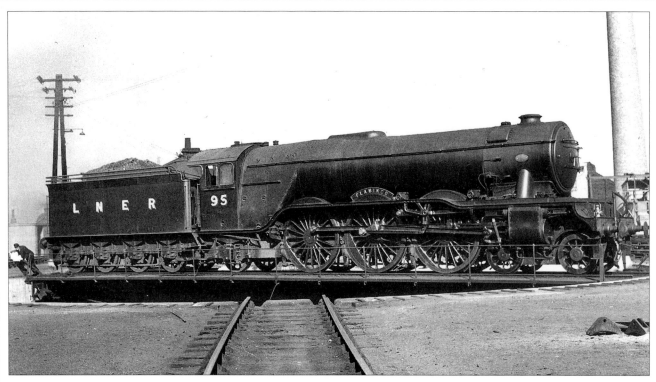

An unusually good shot of an A3 in black livery. FLAMINGO is being turned on the Haymarket turntable. As the engine was numbered 558 in March 1946 and then 95 in May of the same year, and regained LNER apple green in August 1947, the date must lay within that 12 months. Boiler: 94A(9450) Tender: GN (5224) J. Robertson, The Transport Treasury.

APPEARANCES
Bearing in mind that many readers will find innocent pleasure in tracking the various changes to the basic design in the illustrations, I will describe briefly the visual changes that have taken place over the years and how they may be identified. The photographs have been extensively captioned and I hope that this will be of interest, to complement a magnificent collection.

SMOKEBOX
Starting at the front of the engine, the smokebox door remained as a typical Doncaster door throughout with two long hinges, closed by the usual dart locating in a crossbar in the centre and secured at the centre by two handles as usual. Door stops were not provided at first but as the result of an accident in 1930 to a fireman, Gresley agreed to modify the hinges to prevent the door swinging too far. The baffle liner behind the door was attached by countersunk rivets pre-war, then by welded bolts, neither of which could be seen. Post-war, snap head rivets were used, and these could be seen. No.2581 NEIL GOW was fitted with a smokebox door wheel for a while before the war and several photographs of it exist.

NUMBERS AND ALLOCATIONS
Numbers were carried on the buffer beam until nationalisation, when a numberplate was attached to the door above the top hinge. No.60054 PRINCE OF WALES was the first A3 to emerge with one. Cowlairs and Darlington overhauled the Pacifics in their Areas until 1930, and there were

Compare changes. FLAMINGO at Haymarket again, this time with its crew posing, October 12th 1958. Their names are unknown but they appear to be Haymarket men, about to take the A3 back to her home town. Behind the A3 is Haymarket's only Class A2/3 Pacific, No.60519 HONEYWAY looking, to southern eyes, remarkably clean. On the right is one of the Waverley pilots, J83 No.68457. Boiler: 107 (29283) Tender: A4 non-corridor (5637) W. Hermiston, The Transport Treasury.

No.60035 WINDSOR LAD in apple green, with her BR number, alongside Gateshead's BITTERN at the west end of Haymarket, October 30ᵗʰ 1949. Boiler: 94A(8084) Tender: Non corridor (5567) J. Robertson, The Transport Treasury.

slight differences in the livery. Darlington described the engines as being "Class 4.6.2" on the buffer beam while Cowlairs omitted any classification. Doncaster put the appropriate "Class A1" or "Class A3" on the buffer beam, but in March 1938 dropped the word "Class" and added the shed allocation instead. Again, on nationalisation, the shed allocation took the form of the familiar elliptical plate low on the door. At Darlington it was the normal practice to paint the outside cylinders of locomotives with a lined apple green panel, but I can find no examples of A1s and A3s so treated.

LAMP IRONS
The top lamp iron posed problems for the Motive Power authorities in later years. There was originally a fifth lamp iron front and rear for a GNR headcode, but this was removed as it was not normally used. Fine detail, perhaps, but the attempts to improve matters altered the appearance of the locomotives quite radically. A number, ten I believe, were fitted with a door in which the handrail had been repositioned very slightly higher, requiring the numberplate introduced by BR to be fixed below instead of above. Of course repositioning may have been the result of a simple repair to an otherwise sound door, but complaints had previously been made by firemen having to reach up in poor light or wet weather. Drivers were also annoyed by the turbulence the headboard caused around the chimney, dragging the exhaust down and endangering visibility.

By the 1960s the shadow of overhead electrification had fallen across the railway, and it was essential for the safety of staff to educate them as to the lethal dangers of climbing above footplate level. What had been the accepted practice hitherto was no longer permitted. Management also took a more serious view of the dangers of staff having to clamber around on smooth and slippery locomotives without adequate foothold or protection. Warning notices or "flashes" were fixed to the locomotives. At the same time that German deflectors were fitted, two of the surviving A3s, CAPTAIN CUTTLE and DIAMOND JUBILEE, were fitted with a bracket carrying the numberplate on the top door hinge strap, with the handrail above and the lamp iron lowered to roughly where the numberplate used to be. Shortly after, the lamp iron was lowered further and the handrail was replaced with two short half rails each side. Twenty-six locomotives got the new arrangement.

CHIMNEY
The chimney of the prototype A1 was reduced in height by 3ins, in common with her sisters, to meet loading gauge restrictions in the north. Exhaust arrangements had since been varied from time to time but the outward appearance of the engines was not otherwise affected. It remained unaltered, except in the cases of Nos.2747 and 2751, until the advent of double chimneys in 1958. A variety of chimneys and smokebox arrangements were used on these two A3s between October 1931 and 1934, after which CORONACH reverted to normal. The double chimney was lipped as first seen on No.2751 HUMORIST

in 1933, then as a true double chimney in 1937 on the same engine.

The Kylchap double blastpipe and chimney was not necessarily fitted at general overhaul. It was a surprisingly cheap and simple modification, and feasible even at major depots. It was fitted at Doncaster Works both at general overhaul and during inspections and casual repairs. I recall TRACERY on her return from routine examination at Doncaster with a new double blastpipe in July 1958. The driver of the 14.00 "Heart of Midlothian" was however convinced that the A3 ran so well that she must have been fresh from general overhaul, whereas the truth was that she had at least 40,000 miles under her belt!

Smoke deflection was always a problem, but not normally a major one. With the fitting of a double chimney to HUMORIST the problem of deflection became more acute. In February 1938 the ornamental lip was removed from the chimney leaving a double stovepipe, and two small chimneyside deflectors were added. It is doubtful whether this was a satisfactory solution, but war intervened and crews had to make do. In May 1947 the small deflectors were removed and a pair of standard Peppercorn type large deflectors were fitted, and a year later the stovepipe chimney was embellished with a small half-round beading similar to the last A2 being built and the new A1s. The more aesthetically pleasing double chimney was produced for the A1s in April 1951, virtually identical with the 1933 model, and fitted to HUMORIST, so completing the circle of nearly twenty years!

The magnificent Haymarket A3 twins, E99 at this time and 100 behind. CALL BOY was at Haymarket in 1948-49, carrying the temporary BR number. Boiler: 94A(8223) Tender: Non corridor (5568) J. Robertson, The Transport Treasury.

FRONT VIEW

The buffer beam was a distinctive feature of the A1s and A3s. It was originally rectangular but in trial running on the NE main line it was found necessary that, to clear sharply curved station platforms such as Newcastle Central, notches had to be cut off the bottom corners – the tale of No.1481 has already been related. All new construction featured notching albeit not so large, and the rest of the GNR A1s were adapted retrospectively. The buffers used were Spencer's double buffers, which were smaller than Group Standard.

Below the saddle was an inspection access to the conjugating levers and bearings. From 1933 a cover plate was fitted to prevent the ingress of smokebox ash and char. Footsteps were not originally provided at the front end of Nos.1470 and 1471, but a simple step was provided on Nos.1472-1481 when being built. The front of a large engine such as an A1 or A3 was not a safe place, especially if the smokebox door was being opened, and it was all too easy to lose one's footing or slip. Firemen needing access to the front of the engine when not in a platform had to climb along the side from the cab or use natural athleticism! This step was immediately behind the notching of the buffer beam referred to above, and was probably foul of the structure gauge north of Shaftholme Junction. This would explain the progressive removal of this useful aid in mounting the front of the engine. The Motive Power

authorities eventually complained and full size plate steps, set back, were added as engines were overhauled from 1935. Two sets of guard irons were fitted, one on the bogie frame and the second larger set on the main frame. The larger irons were removed in the 1950s.

ATC/AWS

The leading bogie axleboxes were protected from road dust by plate shields. These became very much part of the appearance of the A1s and A3s but they were gradually removed in the 1950s when several Eastern Region engines were fitted with BR Automatic Train Control receivers. An inclined plate protected the front coupling from swinging and damaging the receiver. Later, ATC was renamed Automatic Warning System (AWS) and the receivers were fitted to all of the class except the four Canal engines at Carlisle. The Waverley route was not fitted with AWS as the traffic levels did not warrant it and the intention in any case was to close the line eventually.

NE AREA PACIFICS

The NE engines, Nos.2568-2582, were equipped with the Westinghouse air brake on the tender and with connecting pipes as an option for the train. The pump was carried on the right-hand side of the boiler. As the LNER adopted the vacuum brake as standard, the equipment was removed between 1933 and 1935. The NE A1s were also fitted with the Raven Fog-

Signalling apparatus that was in use between York and Croxdale, near Durham. When through operation to Newcastle and then Edinburgh became possible, the NE Area insisted that Southern and Scottish Area engines should be compliant, and a total of seventy A1s and A3s were eventually fitted with the equipment. The Raven system was discontinued in October 1933 and so it was also removed between 1933 and 1935.

Whilst on the subject of brakes and warning systems, it is relevant to mention the Hudd system, though the equipment was not normally visible. It was a non-contact system and the father of the present AWS, although one has to say that the *grand*father was the GWR contact system. The development of the Hudd system was given great impetus by the outcome of the Castlecary collision on December 10th 1937, near Glasgow, when No.2744 GRAND PARADE collided with a stopping train at full speed in a snowstorm. Six Pacifics were fitted, but war intervened and the equipment was removed in 1943.

SMOKEBOX SIDE

Moving round to the smokebox, an obvious change from the A1 to the A3 was the fitting of an enlarged superheater header, which necessitated two raised casings either side of the smokebox ahead of the front tubeplate. When No.2562 ISINGLASS was built, it was fitted with a type E superheater and tested. The volume of the larger superheater was such that

No.60087 BLENHEIM in BR livery. It looks very much like the BR dark blue but I could be wrong! The date would be about 1951 in that case. The location is unknown but it doesn't look like Haymarket. Boiler: 94A(9121) Tender: Non corridor (5572).

it was necessary to fit two anti-vacuum or snifting valves, one on each casing. These were removed in August 1930. The snifting valves were normally placed behind the chimney. In passing, one not knowing these locomotives might consider the forward positioning of the double chimney both unbalanced and inelegant. However, unless there was to be major and expensive surgery on the boiler and front tubeplate, the position was determined by the presence of the header and the need to get access to it. The ability of boilersmiths to install a steamtight header and superheater elements in such a confined space always seemed to call for a remarkable agility, if not imagination, to me.

As built, the inclined casings carried the main steam pipes between the superheater header from where they left the smokebox, and the cylinders. Whilst the steam pipes were anything but straight, the casings of the Doncaster built engines were straight. Those built by North British had a small elbow bend visible just above running board level, but it was hidden with the introduction of the enlarged flat casings below, consequent upon fitting with long travel valve gear.

VALVE GEAR
Looking below, these flat casings originally ran alongside the smokebox saddle of the A1 back to the first splasher. This gave access to the top of the combination lever and the exhaust passages. When No.4477 GAY CRUSADER was modified with improved valve events, the casing was

not altered and, despite being modified again with the later design with long valve travel, her appearance in this respect was not changed until later, in 1933. When No.2555 CENTENARY was modified, the casing was extended outwards from the saddle and backwards beyond the splasher to the rise in the running plate over the leading coupled wheel. Now it was more visible, and from this one can tell whether an engine had original or long valve travel. The extended casing gave room for the longer combination lever to operate and be lubricated.

BOILER
Moving to the boiler, this was the principal means of telling an A1 from an A3 at a glance. The A1 180psi Diagram 94 boiler had a dome and no

An official depiction of CALL BOY with double chimney, A4 boiler and AWS at Doncaster, with the background painted out. I assume the date to be July 1958. Why did Doncaster Paintshop roof leak over the years, I wonder? One could see a freshly painted locomotive inside, a vision to delight the eye, but by the time it had moved outside and transferred "across the road" to Carr Loco, there were the tell tale streaks of rust, etc. They were easily cleaned off, but I suppose nobody was there to add that finishing touch. Boiler: 107 (29306) Tender: Non-corridor (5568).

FLYING SCOTSMAN in an official view, again after general overhaul and repainting, and cleaning too, this time. The later totem and the single chimney pinpoint that date as July 1957, shortly before my own remarkable journey with her. Boiler: 94A (27011) Tender: A4 non-corridor (5640).

superheater header casings. The 220psi boiler of 1927 was classified as a Diagram 94HP boiler, and retained a dome but had the header casings. In 1934 the last batch of A3s had a different type of steam collector, known because of its unusual shape as the "banjo dome". This boiler was classified Diagram 94A, the need for a different description arising from both the different type of steam collector and the use of a 7ins main steam pipe instead of 5ins, almost doubling its cross sectional area. The boilers were essentially the same shell outwardly except for those features mentioned. Apart from the boilers ordered with each batch of new locomotives, batches of spare boilers were ordered over the years from the 1930s onwards, usually Diagram 94A, but post-war also Diagram 107. With the rebuilding of the A1s, the Diagram 94 boilers slowly disappeared in the 1940s. Edward Thompson exceptionally ordered a batch of nine new 94HP boilers in May 1944, preferring the appearance of a simple dome, but presumably with the smaller and less effective main steam pipe as well.

In the 1950s, the A4 Diagram 107 boiler was successfully brought into use on Haymarket's illustrious No.60099 CALL BOY and from that time production of the Diagram 94A boilers ceased. The Diagram 107 boiler was used with the working pressure set at 220psi on the A3s, although

The front of SPEARMINT in her last months. The location is not given, but it might be Perth, where one could take such a view. The old girl is in a poor state, black and uncared for. From this vantage point one could see the hatches and covers to enable the inner workings to be examined, oiled and adjusted. It is also an unusually good view of how the snifting valve was mounted, the chimney and the cover to the valve gear. Not a picture to be happy about. Boiler: 94A(27063) Tender: Non corridor (5566) The Transport Treasury.

BAYARDO, having reversed on to the Haymarket turntable on August 19th 1950. The A3 was looking clean which, considering it had three months since overhaul for Carlisle to let it get dirty, makes a pleasant sight. At the repair in May 1950 she was turned out with the diagram 94HP boiler off BROWN JACK, which was ordered in 1944 by Edward Thompson, who preferred the traditional dome rather than the banjo. There were always pieces of railway furniture to obstruct the photographer from finding the perfect composition, and John Robertson clearly had trouble with a telegraph pole and the turntable vacuum engine here! Boiler: 94HP (27066) Tender: GN (5288) J. Robertson, The Transport Treasury.

when the boiler was lifted and repaired by the Boiler Shop at Doncaster, several went back on to A4s working at 250psi! The bulk of the A3s ran till the end with Diagram 94A boilers, and although the pre-war Diagram 94HP boilers were eventually replaced, Thompson's nine 94HP boilers continued, and it was possible to see an A3 with a domed boiler right through till the end. Doncaster boilers lasted well. The engines fitted with Diagram 107 boilers can be recognised immediately by the firebox inspection doors. On a 94A these were roughly level, whereas on a 107 they were inclined upwards towards the cab. Also the banjo dome on a 107 boiler sat further forward to clear the A4 firebox combustion chamber but it is difficult to see that difference.

Tracking down the boilers used at any one time with the aid of Willie Yeadon's Register is difficult, given the occasional tendency to hold a repaired boiler as a spare for a period. It was made more difficult at the turn of the 1950s when BR, in its infinite wisdom, decided to renumber the boilers from the Doncaster series (7500-10000 approx.) into a BR series (27000+). As far as I can deduce, this was done quite randomly, and unless the renumbering is specifically detailed, there is a clear break in boiler numbering.

CAB CONTROLS
Whether the locomotive was driven from the right as were the A1s originally, or the left as the A3s, is apparent from the position of the reversing rod which passed under the firebox cladding before running under the running board to the reversing shaft. That fitted by North British to its A1s was the Darlington version with a dip below the Westinghouse pump. The Doncaster version was a long heavy rod that ran for most of its length at the lower level; to ease dismantling and re-erecting, it was later made into two halves. The Darlington rod survived to the end of the A3s on seven or eight ex-NE Area engines. Post-war, it was decided to extend the maximum cut-off to 75%, but the change was not normally visible. Similarly, it was decided to convert the former A1 class engines to left-hand drive in the early 1950s. One wonders why it took so long to make a simple change of great benefit to the driver, who hitherto had to drive at speed, dependent much of the time on his fireman checking that the signal was still clear. On the driver's side, the steam supplies to the blower were in a tube below the boiler handrail. Immediately under the cab an external rod and crank operated the drop grate section, which was useful in cleaning

the fire and dropping clinkered fire, always a problem with poorer coal. This was under the fireman's side of the cab. Below the cab one could see the trailing axle with its Cortazzi axleboxes.

SPEEDOS
Speedometers were fitted to some engines before the war, but were then removed. Before the war and occasionally post-war, a speedometer or Flaman speed recording machine was specially fitted, usually for test running. A distinctive bracket under the running board on the fireman's side by the rear coupled wheel enabled the speedometer drive to be taken off the rear connecting rod bearing. The Flaman recorder bracket is visible in the illustration of TAGALIE at Craigentinny. Not only did it display the speed but provided a record of the speeds attained in service, sometimes to the driver's embarrassment. It was not until the late 1950s that the engines were fitted with the Smith-Stone speedometer as a result of several accidents involving misjudgement of speed. This was a fairly reliable instrument usually reading within about +5% inaccuracy but it indicated only the speed and did not record. It was operated off the rear crankpin of the third coupled axle

SIR VISTO, fresh from Doncaster Paintshop, posed outside in light steam on July 26th 1955. It would have been handed over to Carr Loco the following day to start test running to Retford, Lincoln or usually Barkston triangle, before running-in proper and returning to Carlisle Canal. No.60068 was the last of the A1s, by then classified as A10s, reboilered almost in the last days of the LNER's existence. As has been mentioned several times, Carlisle A3s were among the rarest visitors to the south, and when one was seen south of Newcastle, it was a photograph not to be missed, especially as the engine was usually freshly repainted, as here. Carlisle and Scottish A3s very occasionally worked through to London before the 1939-45 war on football specials, but after, one had to rely on the beneficence of the Doncaster Shedmaster or Running Foreman. Boiler: 94A (27036) Tender: GN (5224) P.J. Lynch.

again, but this time on the driver's side.

TENDERS
The locomotives were coupled to one of four different types of tender. The tenders of the A1s were all of the GN type with coal rails. With the construction of the ten corridor tenders in 1928, it was unnecessary to build any extra ones for the first batch of A3s, and the engines emerged with either a corridor tender or a displaced GN tender. The eight new engines of the second batch of A3s in 1930 were coupled to a non-corridor variant of the high sided tender in most cases, or to a corridor tender in the case of Nos.2795 and 2796. The same approach was used for the nine A3s of 1934/35. When the ten corridor tenders were removed from the A1s and A3s, the replacements were A3 high sided tenders that had been built for the five Raven Pacifics and five A4 versions of the high-sided tender. The latter differed from the A3 tender in having no external beading. These tenders survived to withdrawal. Apart from the GN tender, the corridor tender and its two derivatives differed significantly in weight as will be seen in the dimensions of Appendix A. It seems probable that there was a slight difference in their capacities, since

their construction was similar. There were some locomotives that changed tenders almost every time they went for general overhaul, and others which emerged with the same one, and again one can track them through Yeadon's remarkable Register. Only one, ROBERT THE DEVIL, kept the same tender throughout its career. The GN tenders carried their numberplate at the rear under the coal rails, while all of the high sided tenders carried their numberplates high over the coal door, on the footplate.

LIVERY
The livery of the first A1s was the standard GNR livery of apple green lined out in black and white and edged with olive green. This, apart from the edging colour, was adopted for the LNER passenger livery and the A1s and A3s, all built in LNER ownership, carried this livery until the 1939-45 war. The NE engines were overhauled at Darlington until 1930, and that works continued to use a slightly different shade of apple green. In the war years, unlined black was used, with restoration to lined apple green in 1946. With the introduction of British Railways ownership, experimental liveries were tried, No.60091 CAPTAIN CUTTLE being the guinea pig, unhappily, with a purplish hue,

lined out first in yellow, followed by a modified lining of cream and red. Six more A3s were similarly painted, Nos.60036, 60045, 60071, 60074, 60075 and 60084. The standard BR dark blue livery was introduced from 1949, but it did not last well and in 1951, probably at the urging of voices west of London, the dark green of the heavy mixed traffic locomotives was extended to all large express and mixed traffic locomotives. With a large class of locomotives the period between the first engine and the last receiving a new livery could extend to two-three years and the two Darlington pilots, as mentioned, were never painted blue, but went from apple to dark green.

During their lifetime, the locomotives have carried different arrangements of numbers and company initials on the cab side and tenders as their ownership changed. So GNR changed to L&NER, then to simpler LNER, and then to British Railways in 1948 followed by the use of the two totems representing BR, known to the irreverent as the Ferret and Dartboard followed by the Beer Label. During the war years the LNER initials were used later, reduced to NE as an economy. The Company used a plain block capital font for its livery and nameplates until the 1930s when Medium Gill Sans was introduced as its replacement. Only the last batch of A3s received Gill Sans nameplates, although one subsequent replacement, BLINK BONNY, was a Gill Sans engine. Curiously, when TAGALIE was given her new nameplate, Doncaster had reverted to the old font. The nameplates were very heavy brass castings mounted over the driving wheel splasher, attached by means of a base flange. Early namplates started to crack, and the casting was strengthened together stiffening ribs added at the rear. The works plate was also a brass plate attached to the smokebox side, elliptical in the case of Doncaster, and a round North British works plate for Nos.2563-2582. The NB works plates were removed and not replaced. The Doncaster plates were moved to the cabside, as on the A4s, when the trough deflectors were fitted.

The locomotives carried, essentially, two numbers during their careers. The GNR engines, with the whole of the GNR stock, had 3,000 added to give their LNER number. The rest were numbered as LNER stock in the peculiarly random fashion of the Company. In the Thompson renumbering of 1946, after a false start with some twenty engines being numbered in the 500 series, they received their final numbers. On nationalisation they were initially tagged with an "E", and then with all ex-LNER engines had their running numbers increased by 60,000. One of the idiosyncrasies of the LNER was the use of a different "6" or "9" from the Gill font for numberplates. This was corrected later, the anomaly no doubt caused by the Casting Shop using incorrect (old?) characters to make up their numberplate patterns. There were some other minor alterations to cab sides and handrails, but I have described the principal visible means of identifying the state of the locomotive during its career.

MILEAGES

Of the vast amount of published detail in these works and others, the only figures that appeared to be missing from the wealth of material in the public domain were the individual locomotive mileages. The engines were nominated for general overhaul once they had run 80,000 miles. The Shopping Bureau at the Works was usually quite inflexible, for the simple reason that there were such things as budgets. Each overhaul was a significant cost and the Works Manager could not afford to repair every run-down machine at the drop of a hat. On the other hand a Shedmaster could be left with the impossible task of running the qualifying total mileage with a locomotive that few would take. The Pacifics were overhauled at Doncaster Works in the main, although casual repairs and modifications were done at Darlington, Gateshead and Cowlairs. In her last months PRINCE PALATINE achieved a unique visit to Inverurie Works for an unclassified repair, surely the largest locomotive by far to be repaired there.

Fortunately I was sufficiently inquisitive a long while ago to purchase copies of drawings and to ascertain the figures from the Eastern Region PR&PO as they then stood. However, since then two sets, one from copies of the individual Works Accountants' letters and the other from the "Gresley Observer" in its infancy have surfaced, and it will surprise nobody that they all disagree at times. They refer to slightly different dates, but the differences cannot explained just by their recording dates. Which is remarkable seeing that they come from a common source, ultimately.

An unusual view at Doncaster Works showing the similarity in the A3 and A4 cabs. By that time the concentration of Pacifics at some sheds, notably Top Shed, led to the Valves and Pistons examinations being carried out at Doncaster Works. Obviously there was an expertise in the Works that was not always available outside, and this is the reason for ISINGLASS and SILVER LINK being here. It had the advantage that other smaller jobs such as fitting the double chimney or trough deflectors could be considered by the Works if there was manpower and time available. Here one can see the brake pipes, coupling bars and safety chains that kept the engine and tender together in extremis. The AWS battery box is under the fireman's seat in each case, and the timing and AWS reservoir are under the dragbox, the strengthened rear frame structure by which the engine hauled its train. The purpose of the timing reservoir, with a distant or colour light signal at caution, is to provide a delay – fourteen seconds, I remember – for the driver to apply the brake. If he had not acted, the AWS system would take over from him and destroy down to five inches of vacuum, a heavy brake application! Notice, model makers, that the works plate of the A3, moved because the trough deflectors are now fitted, is slightly higher on the cab side than the A4. The date is January 14th 1962. Boiler: 107 (29295) Tender: Would have been GN (5231) P.B. Booth, Neville Stead Collection.

A word of caution, indeed several words of caution. Locomotive mileages were aggregated by the Works Accountant before and during Nationalisation from the drivers' tickets. The latter was a return completed by the driver on completion of a turn of duty. The aggregate mileage was the means by which mileage related inspections and overhauls were identified. Although given down to the last mile, it was not that accurate and probably not so to more than the nearest few hundred miles overall at best. These can be accepted as a practical basis, although if they were not accurate, it would not be obvious to the Works Accountant. He had bigger fish to fry. Of course the figures emerged some while after the mileage had been achieved, and so the Shedmaster had to anticipate, or keep a check on his locomotives independently as at least one chose to do. The figures are vulnerable like any other statistic to mistakes by driver, the recorder, and the typist who included them in various letters.

The situation was complicated by a BTC decision to abandon steam locomotive mileage recording in 1962. Steam locomotives surviving beyond October 1963 had their mileages estimated. Comparison between the mileages for March and December 1962 show some remarkable achievements in nine months, but allowance must be made for mileage incurred but not booked. Locomotives withdrawn before 1961-62 have a reasonably accurate recorded mileage, but those withdrawn after 1962 do not. One might hazard a guess at their average mileage but with the decline in steam operation at that time that can prove difficult. Haymarket for example, sent many of their Pacifics to St. Margaret's, of which a number subsequently went into store at Dalry Road, then Bathgate and other places before withdrawal. Later, Gateshead did the same.

Nevertheless the list of mileages is not above the occasional query. One list, for example, shows No.60036 COLOMBO comfortably exceeding two million miles, a score which would require near miraculous availability and impeccable reliability. Therefore I have quoted the lower figure shown, which bears sensible comparison with the rest of the batch. The four Carlisle locomotives showed unusually low mileages until increased by the amount accumulated in LM Region operation and recorded separately. Two further engines stand out as having an incorrect mileage, Gateshead's GLADIATEUR no less, and ST. GATIEN. When the performance of the rest of the original Gateshead batch, Nos.2568-2577, is considered, it is uniformly high, and they seem to be well adrift. The correct mileage for No.60073 is actually 2.3m miles as shown and not 1.3m, no doubt a simple typing mistake since it has been repeated several times. No.60070 has been corrected to the figure shown in the "Gresley Observer", but it still seems about 300-350,000 miles too low. Two small mistakes maybe, but something not calculated to instil confidence.

I have quoted the dates given in Willie Yeadon's "Yeadon's Register of LNER Locomotives" for entry into traffic and withdrawal, although as he states, there may be some difference between the dates recorded as leaving works and the date entering into traffic. If a locomotive ran hot on its first trip to Retford or Lincoln, for example, it may have returned to Works. And of course locomotives were taken out of use before they were actually overhauled or withdrawn in some cases.

In the photographs I have identified the date, the livery, boiler carried and the tender attached at the time, as far as possible. I have relied entirely on the date quoted, if any, by the photographer, although experience has shown that to be not entirely wise. All authors of such histories must be haunted by the thought that they have made a misjudgement that, after publication and in retrospect, is both obvious and ridiculous. If I have, I apologise.

DIAMOND JUBILEE standing at Top Shed waiting for its turn at the Cenotaph. A wagon loaded with coal is being winched up to replenish supplies. The front of the A3 is a good study, being in its final form with the numberplate on the top hinge strap lowered top lamp iron and lowered handrail. Later, A3s were fitted with a divided handrail. One can also see the inspection hole for the conjugated valve gear, which after 1933 was fitted with a sliding cover to prevent the ingress of ash. In the right background is the N2 0-6-2T preserved by the Gresley Society Trust at Loughborough, No.69523. No date is given but she is a Grantham engine and it must be at least 1962. Boiler: 94A(27086) Tender: A4 Non-corridor (5644) B. Richardson, The Transport Treasury.

LEMBERG, the old Doncaster favourite, now one of Darlington's pilots, which is probably where she was photographed, on August 17th 1958. She was repainted at overhaul in January of that year, and is still in very clean condition. Boiler: 94A (27028) Tender: GN (5228) J. Robertson, The Transport Treasury.

FLYING FOX, posed on the new turntable at Kings Cross, in original condition, as yet unnamed. The date must be 1923-24 to judge from the lettering and GNR numbering, and therefore the engine has not yet had its first overhaul, and the boiler and tender must be the originals. Boiler: 94 (7696) Tender: GN (5226) G. Goslin, The Gresley Society.

The first of the final batch, WINDSOR LAD, in its official photograph, a hardy annual but a good one. Boiler: 94A (8776) Tender: Non corridor (5567).

SALMON TROUT, one of the 1934 quartet, which were long term residents at Haymarket from new until the exodus to St. Margarets in 1960 to make way for the mediocre 2000HP diesels. She was a very rare sight in the south, but survived to become one of the final trio of A3s at the end of 1965. The date is May 6th 1937. Boiler: 94A (8782) Tender: GN (5226) R.J. Buckley, Initial Photographics.

The fourth member of the quartet was LNER No.2508 BROWN JACK, photographed at Craigentinny carriage sidings. The A4 non-corridor tender was only attached between overhauls in April 1937 and April 1938, which fixes the date of the picture. Boiler: 94A (8784) Tender: Non corridor (5641) J. Robertson, The Transport Treasury.

What was once BLINK BONNY when it entered the Works at Doncaster, and hopefully would be once more when it left. It has been stripped and its components have gone to the various specialist departments such as the Boiler Shop and the Wheel Shop. Many consumable components would have been scrapped and replaced with new, such as axleboxes. All that remains are just the frames as a sort of boilerless Bo-Bo on accommodation bogies. They will be taken into the shops, cleaned and work will start on any remedial repairs such as welding, etc. Then the locomotive will be reconstructed with new or fettled components, a repaired boiler probably off an earlier engine, retyred and turned wheels, and eventually coupled to a tender and repainted. The A3 was fitted with AWS and left-hand drive prior to stripping. An interesting photograph if one has never seen an A3 stripped right down. The date must be February 1960, since that is the only time when BLINK BONNY and K3 No.61956 were at Doncaster Works together. Boiler: 94A (27056 removed and 27033 to take its place) Tender: Non corridor (5580). B. Richardson, The Transport Treasury.

Chapter Seven
THE A3 PORTFOLIO

60035. As No.35, WINDSOR LAD stands outside Haymarket shed at Edinburgh. Willie Hermiston gives no date for this well-nigh perfect shed shot of one of the more famous Scottish A3s, but clearly it is post-1946 LNER numbering; the engine was released to traffic in apple green livery on 3 September 1947. Boiler: 94A(9121) Tender: Non-corridor (5567) W. Hermiston, The Transport Treasury.

60035. By March 1st 1959 WINDSOR LAD has BR dark green, double chimney and AWS. She (he?) is standing at Haymarket with Carlisle Canal's B1 No.61217 and Heaton's No.60088 BOOK LAW. She was one of the least common visitors to the capital, a very rare sight indeed south of Doncaster. Boiler: 94A(27058) Tender: Non-corridor (5567) J. Robertson, The Transport Treasury.

60036. COLOMBO was a Tyneside engine for many years before moving to Leeds. She was one of the multi-hued A3s, changing from LNER apple green to experimental purple in July 1948 and then to BR Caledonian blue exactly one year later before becoming BR green in December 1951. In this view on the Haymarket turntable she is in the experimental purple livery, which extended down to the panel on the cylinders, as in Darlington practice. Doncaster always painted the cylinders black and lined them out. Boiler: 94A(9511) Tender: GN (5227) J. Robertson, The Transport Treasury.

60037. A sight for sore eyes. HYPERION at Haymarket, her apple green paintwork beautifully cleaned, prior to running down to Waverley. I suspect she is to work the Royal train or at least stand pilot, or has just done so, by the look of the burnished metalwork. Condensation on the tender sides has outlined the water space and one can see her shed allocation clearly on the buffer beam. The boiler identifies the date between July 1947 and June 1950, and I would put it at November 1948, fresh from general overhaul. The late Charles Meacher told me that the driver is Peter Robertson. Boiler: 94HP(27027) Tender: GN (5261) J. Patterson, The Transport Treasury.

60037. HYPERION in Dundee Tay Bridge station on a sunny afternoon, May 13th 1951, with an up train of mixed stock for Edinburgh. The Class B headcode was unusual for an express locomotive but certainly not unheard of. Tay Bridge was not the easiest station for photography and this is an unusual view. The enlarged covers to the modified valve gear can be seen clearly. Boiler: 94A(10541) Tender: GN (5285) John F. Aylard.

60037. HYPERION at Haymarket having just returned from general overhaul at Doncaster Works, when she received a Kylchap double chimney and one of the nine 94HP boilers ordered by Thompson. The date is October 19th 1958. Boiler: 94HP(27066) Tender: GN (5276) J. Robertson, The Transport Treasury.

60038. Gateshead's FIRDAUSSI was one of the more camera-shy A3s. This is in her early years, as 2503 on a down express emerging from Hadley North Tunnel at Ganwick. At a guess, it is summer, and the train is an early evening departure from London. Like the up "Flying Scotsman", the first vehicle is a full brake (BG). Boiler: 94A(8779) Tender: Non-corridor (5571 or 83) Gresley Society Trust.

60039. SANDWICH was originally a Gateshead engine, one of the last batch of nine shared between Gateshead and Haymarket, but it soon migrated south in exchange for the third A4, SILVER KING, which then stood pilot for the "Silver Jubilee" A4. She was a regular sight at the south end of the East Coast main line, and was regarded as one of the best. In LNER green, she is passing Greenwood signalbox with an up express on July 29th 1948, three weeks after general overhaul at Doncaster Works. The train was probably the predecessor of the "Northumbrian", approx. 10.00 from Newcastle. Boiler: 94A(9208) Tender: Non-corridor (5573) Cawston Bequest, Canon Brian C. Bailey collection.

60039. SANDWICH gingerly starts the down "Yorkshire Pullman" from King's Cross Platform 6; she received deflectors in June 1961, so the date is probably later in that summer. She still has her high-sided non-corridor tender of many years, No.5573 and is also fitted with a Diagram 107 boiler, identifiable by the different position of the inspection holes. Boiler: 107(27968) Tender: Non-corridor (5573) Derek A. Potton, The Transport Treasury.

60039. SANDWICH in her final state with double chimney, deflectors, AWS, Diagram 107 boiler, but with the same high sided tender as ever. She is of course, on the down Scots Goods, No.266 down, on the down main south of Harringay having been turned out at Finsbury Park. How many passenger services, let alone a humble fast freight, could boast an engine in such superb condition, I wonder? Boiler: 107(27968) Tender: Non-corridor (5573) Peter Groom.

60040. CAMERONIAN heads a down express near Grantshouse, climbing the 1 in 200 to Penmanshiel Tunnel. The underbridge is one of those washed away in the 1948 rainstorms. It is an LMSR reinforced concrete (RC) design as most were, and can be distinguished by the use of RC to form the parapet handrails. Date June 20th 1953. Boiler: 94A(27001) Tender: GN (5253) J. Robertson, The Transport Treasury.

60040. CAMERONIAN standing as southbound pilot at Darlington, now in her final form. She was a Gateshead engine for almost her entire existence, apart from spells at Darlington. This excellent study shows the final arrangement of smokebox door handrails, lamp irons and numberplate. Boiler: 94A(27001) Tender: GN (5253) The Transport Treasury.

60041. Another Scottish engine for the whole of her existence, most of it at Haymarket shed, was SALMON TROUT. With HYPERION standing behind on September 29th 1957 'the trout' eases on to the turntable at Haymarket. Boiler: 94A(27082) Tender: GN (5272) J. Robertson, The Transport Treasury.

60041. SALMON TROUT pounds up the last few yards of the 1 in 96 of Cockburnspath Bank before reaching the tunnel with an up express. The tunnel under Penmanshiel Moor penetrated a layer of glacial debris that is loose and wet. The channel on the right takes the ground water away from the tunnel, while the large stack of bricks is evidence of a prospective weekend or two of repairs to the tunnel lining in the near future by the District Engineer at Edinburgh. The date is not given but is probably early 1950s to judge from No.60041's train and her condition. The leading coach appears to be a Gresley "Tourist" coach. Boiler: 94A(27067) Tender: GN (5272) J. Robertson, Transport Treasury.

60042. SINGAPORE at the southern end of the East Coast main line, heading a parcels train on a Sunday morning, September 14th 1958, south of Ponsbourne Tunnel. It may well be the uniquely numbered No.1 up, a York-King's Cross parcels train which ran only on Sundays. All services were diverted via the New Line due to quadrupling at Potters Bar on that weekend. I suspect from her ex-works condition that she was in fact running in from Doncaster shed rather than her home shed. The double chimney had just been fitted. Boiler 94A(27024) Tender: GN (5260) John F. Aylard.

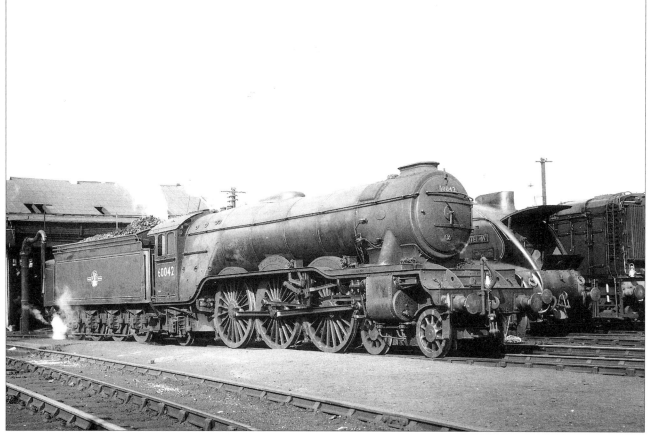

60042. SINGAPORE, the holder of the record time from Newcastle, now with a double chimney, stands at Haymarket between Peppercorn A1 MARMION from Gateshead and the home shed's A4 WILLIAM WHITELAW. Boiler: 94A(27024) Tender: GN (5272) Date Sept 6th, 1959. J. Robertson, The Transport Treasury.

60043. A magnificent needle-sharp photograph of the last A3 to be built, (other than the replacement No.2744 of 1938) BROWN JACK, on an up express at Seton Crossing, near Prestonpans. She was another of the Haymarket fleet, only leaving there for the other side of Edinburgh when the end of steam came. She was used with distinction on the non-stop "Flying Scotsman" before the A4s displaced the A3s in 1937. Date August 6th 1950. Boiler: 94A(9212) Tender: GN (5256) J. Robertson, The Transport Treasury.

60043. BROWN JACK, heading a Class F slow unbraked freight. The A3s were not unknown on slower freights, but usually running in after repair at works or depot, or putting in their last miles as the halt and the lame in order to satisfy the Shopping Bureau at Doncaster Works. The print gives no hint of where and when, but from the look of the permanent way and the locality, I would plump for a down semi-fitted freight on the Waverley route approaching the outskirts of Edinburgh from the foot of Falahill Bank. The locomotive's livery dates it as between 1948 and early 1950. For those interested in fine detail, the Doncaster reversing rod is clearly visible with the bolted joint midway. Boiler: 94HP(9570) Tender: GN (5256) J. Robertson, The Transport Treasury.

60043. BROWN JACK breasting the summit at the south end of Penmanshiel tunnel with the up "Heart of Midlothian". The 14.00 afternoon expresses between the capital cities were among those named in 1951 for the Festival of Britain in that year, and the name was perpetuated. The engine once again is in magnificent condition having recently been overhauled and painted dark green. The view shows the dust shields in front of the bogie axleboxes so typical of the A3s before AWS was introduced. Date September 17th 1951. Boiler: 94A(27055) Tender: GN (5256) J. Robertson, The Transport Treasury.

60044. MELTON, a grand old Southern Area favourite, in BR blue livery on the 15.50 Kings Cross Leeds and York at Greenwood, June 22nd 1950. Doncaster shed had just taken the duty over from York and she worked it very often at that time. The silvered door hinge straps suggests that the engine had been standing pilot for the Royal Train in the recent past. Boiler: 94A(9984) Tender: GN (5274) Cawston Bequest, Canon Brian C. Bailey collection.

60045. LEMBERG, as LNER No.2544, at the head of the up "Flying Scotsman" pulling away from Grantham during the period when the train was not non-stop. The presence of a Doncaster engine on this train, and a regularly manned one at that, was distinctly unusual and possibly a substitution for a failed locomotive. Dated 1930 by the photographer. Boiler: 94HP(8028), one of the first five 220psi boilers to be built in 1927, Tender: GN (5228) Cawston Bequest, Canon Brian C. Bailey collection.

60045. LEMBERG was moved to the North Eastern Area in 1937 along with a number of A1s from the Southern Area as a result of the influx of new A4s. She drifts down the gradient past Grantshouse with an up express of largely LMSR stock on May 31st 1952. The A3 had been overhauled and repainted in BR dark green a month earlier. Boiler: 94A(27007) Tender: GN (5228) J. Robertson, The Transport Treasury.

60045. LEMBERG at the west end of Haymarket a few weeks later, on July 4th 1952. Since her repair Gateshead seems to be making good use of her on main line work. Boiler: 94A(27007) Tender: GN (5228) J. Robertson, The Transport Treasury.

60046. DIAMOND JUBILEE, in her pre-war condition as an A1, 2545, in the engine bay at the south end of Grantham station, by the Yard box, ready to take over an up service on 31 July 1937. The unfortunate competitor in the 1925 Exchanges, she is in LNER apple green livery and has now been coupled to an A4 non-corridor tender, which she kept until withdrawal. As yet unrebuilt obviously she carries an A1 180psi boiler. Boiler: 94 (7703) Tender: A4 Non-corridor (5644) J. Whaley, The Transport Treasury.

60046. Photographs of expresses at speed down the famous Stoke Bank are uncommon, partly because the speed overtaxed the ability of many camera shutters to 'stop' the subject with the film emulsions of the day, and partly because there was little exhaust in any case. The driver looks as though he has eased the A3, his speed being high enough. The cut-off is shortened. DIAMOND JUBILEE is approaching Little Bytham, probably with the Hull portion of the 9.50 from Leeds on August 5th 1957. Boiler: 94A (27069) Tender: A4 Non-corridor (5644) M. Mensing.

60046. A magnificent study of DIAMOND JUBILEE, nearly a quarter of a century later with a double chimney and trough deflectors but yet the same tender. No date or location is given but she is a Grantham engine and it must be at least 1962. Boiler: 94A(27086) Tender: A4 Non-corridor (5644) Barry Richardson, The Transport Treasury.

60047. DONOVAN was another of Grantham's stalwarts. Here she is in full cry with the down "Northumbrian" just before Christmas 1956, strengthened to fourteen coaches, on the 1 in 200 north of New Southgate. No problems here with smoke deflection! Boiler: 94A(27043) Tender: GN (5280) Peter J. Coster.

60047. An unusual shot at Sandy, with DONOVAN heading an up Newcastle express, probably the relief to the up "Northumbrian". This is where the four tracks converged into the two-track bottleneck that plagued operators for many a long year. The down express is the 13.18 Leeds headed by Peppercorn A1 No.60125 SCOTTISH UNION. On the left is the ex-LMSR Oxford-Cambridge route, now closed. Boiler: 94A (27042), Tender: GN (5280) M. Mensing.

60047. DONOVAN, as many fine express locomotives across BR finished their days, on freight. No.60047 is accelerating her freight away from Peterborough North up the sharp gradient to the Nene Bridge. The headlamps show it as a Class E semi-fitted freight, but it looks like a rake of motley 16 ton mineral wagons. Presumably it had a fitted head of Minfit wagons to qualify as Class E, "Number three-speed" in LNER parlance. Boiler: 94A (27042), Tender: GN (5280) Barry Richardson, The Transport Treasury.

60048. DONCASTER accelerates a train of LMSR stock away from the Nene Bridge, south of Peterborough. The engine is one that was fitted with a double chimney during a minor repair at Doncaster at the end of May 1959 and only ran in this condition for five months. She received small chimneyside wing plates in November of the same year, making the photograph somewhat unusual. Boiler: 94A (27061), Tender: GN (5283) Peter Groom.

60049. In the period 1929-33, when the Revd Arthur Cawston was at Grantham, this was the sort of moody subject he photographed often. GALTEE MORE, LNER No.2548, is "getting hold of them" as she pulls away south after taking over at Grantham. Five miles at 1 in 200 faced an up express pulling out of Grantham which meant that the hard work for the fireman had started even before the loco was coupled on. The year is 1932. Boiler: 94 (7879) Tender: GN (5270) Cawston Bequest, Canon Brian C. Bailey collection.

60049. Many years later, GALTEE MORE waits at King's Cross engine yard to take a down express. She was the first to be fitted with trough deflectors, in October 1960. Boiler: 94A(27005) Tender: GN (5232) P. Ransome-Wallis.

60050. PERSIMMON, in appalling external condition, coasts through the old Peterborough North station with an up express on August 6th 1960. As in the pre-war days, she is a Grantham engine, but there is a world of difference in her appearance now. The smokebox door shows that either the stronger blast has drawn more fines and char through the boiler, or more likely, several people have left the chore of cleaning out the accumulated contents to their successor! Note the fine GNR signalbox. Boiler: 107(29272) Tender: GN (5259) Frank Hornby.

60050. PERSIMMON on shed at Doncaster, May 7th 1960. Boiler: 107(29272) Tender: GN (5259) Frank Hornby.

60051. Post-war, BLINK BONNY was one of the A3s at Leeds (Copley Hill) from 1954 to 1957, although within a month she would have moved to Heaton. She is seen here on August 10th 1957, probably on the first part of the up "West Riding" at Greenwood. The engine was one of ten A3s which had the front numberplate and handrail transposed for no obvious reason. The drainage work for the Widening Project is proceeding apace. Boiler: 94A(27080) Tender: Non-corridor (5580) J. Robertson, The Transport Treasury.

60051. Now transferred to Gateshead, BLINK BONNY has worked the up "Talisman" the previous evening and in early 1958 is returning north on the 11.00 Kings Cross-Glasgow. A 'TSR' (Temporary Speed Restriction) is in force south of New Southgate platforms, and the driver has opened out to recover speed. Boiler: 94A(27080) Tender: Non-corridor (5580) Peter J. Coster.

60051. BLINK BONNY was one of the A3s which enjoyed the dubious privilege of being allocated to Neasden. However, she is looking clean and free from leaks as she heads the up "Master Cutler" at Sudbury Hill. As she was coupled to tender No.5580 in December 1952 the date must lay between then and November 1953 when she went to Grantham. Boiler: 94A(27028) Tender: Non-corridor (5580) N. Spinks, John Aylard Collection.

60052. The A3 that ultimately became the last survivor, PRINCE PALATINE, racing through Haddenham on the GW&GC Joint Section with 12.15 Marylebone-Manchester express. No.60052 spent over six years on the GC Section at Leicester and Neasden, before rejoining her sisters Nos.60051, 60053 and 60058 at Leeds. A splendid shot of a less often photographed engine, taken April 25th 1952, shortly after a general overhaul. Boiler: 94A(27021) Tender: GN (5229) Cawston Bequest, Canon Brian C. Bailey collection.

60052. PRINCE PALATINE brings the up "Master Cutler" into Marylebone, May 12th 1954. Shortly after this the engine was used by Neasden for a spell. Boiler: 94A(27064) Tender: GN (5288) Philip J. Kelley.

60053. SANSOVINO, another of the Copley Hill fleet of the 1950s, approaches Grantham from the south at Saltersford cutting with a down Leeds express, September 8th 1956. The down platform is occupied and the distant is "on". Boiler: 94A(27042) Tender: Non-corridor (5570) Peter Groom.

60053. SANSOVINO had been transferred to Gateshead by June 29th 1958, when it was photographed at Haymarket, where the local enthusiasts surely warmly greeted the stranger. By the look of the list of comments on the right-hand cylinder casing, No.60053 has recently been the subject of close attention by the fitters. Haymarket's A4 No.60031 GOLDEN PLOVER is in the background. Boiler: 94A(27067) Tender: Non-corridor (5570) J. Robertson, The Transport Treasury.

60054. PRINCE OF WALES was one of the first two Pacifics to be reallocated to Copley Hill in order to replace the Ivatt Atlantics, but after the 1939-45 war it became a long-term resident on the GC Section. She was transferred to Top Shed in 1956 with the impending transfer of the GC Section to the LM Region. On April 6th 1957 she is only a month out of works and in good fettle, having been superbly 'worked up' by the Top Shed cleaning gang, ready for the 12.18 "Northumbrian". Boiler: 94A(27024) Tender: GN (5264) A.G. Ellis, The Transport Treasury.

60055. WOOLWINDER eases the 9.18 "White Rose" (a frequent combination in early 1957) out of the old Platform 10 at King's Cross. She was always one of the most hardworking engines post-war and was popular. A London engine, she had returned from a spell at Doncaster previously. Boiler: 107(29322) Tender: GN (5286) John F. Aylard.

60055. WOOLWINDER was an early withdrawal, in September 1961. The first post-war A3 to be fitted with a Kylchap double blastpipe in June 1958, she has a little over three years to run before withdrawal. She was fitted with chimneyside deflectors in October 1959, as were three others, which confirms the date as 1960. She is standing at King's Cross (old) Platform 7 having arrived on an up express. Again, the smokebox door bears signs of overheating. One of the roller-bearing Peppercorn A1s, No.60157 GREAT EASTERN, stands alongside. Boiler: 107(29301) Tender: GN (5286) Prorail UK (Durrant)/The Transport Treasury.

60056. A gloriously atmospheric study of CENTENARY at Newcastle Central, May 16th 1954. No.60056 was the engine selected for timing trials in the early 1950s, having a high mileage, and acquitted herself well. She was by then allocated to Grantham, and in this photo had worked through to Newcastle where she was being relieved. The higher standard of coaching stock makes me suspect that this was the down "Flying Scotsman", and so CENTENARY would have been taking the place of a Peppercorn A1, as often happened when a top link engine was being washed out and examined. Boiler: 94A(27004) Tender: GN (5257) J. Robertson, The Transport Treasury.

60057. ORMONDE was another northward transfer from Grantham in 1939, and went to Haymarket. Originally one of the splendid top link engines at Grantham, she was rarely seen south of Doncaster after transfer. She is seen here at Haymarket between duties, with NEIL GOW and V2 No.60844 behind. No date is given but the early BR totem, 94A boiler and left-hand drive places it between September 1952 and early 1957. Boiler: 94A(27012) Tender: GN (5281) W. Hermiston, The Transport Treasury.

60057. ORMONDE, with the reverser already pulled up, accelerates her Aberdeen express away through Princes St Gardens in Edinburgh. No date is given but it must be the 1953-56 period. Boiler: 94A(27012) Tender: GN (5281) Peter Groom.

60057. ORMONDE, now with a double chimney, waits the right away with the "Talisman". The date must be between January 1960 when the 107 boiler was fitted and September 1961 when deflectors were fitted. As it would be after 20.00 at Newcastle, mid-1960 seems the most likely. Boiler: 107(29290) Tender: GN (5281) The Transport Treasury.

60058. BLAIR ATHOL was another of the Copley Hill fleet that moved to Gateshead, which is why this formerly Southern Area locomotive is at the west end of Haymarket on March 16th 1958. No doubt the new arrivals at the Newcastle sheds were strange sights initially to the locals. A number of A3s were coupled to streamlined non-corridor standard tenders such as No.5643 seen here. Boiler: 94A(27012) Tender: A4 Non-corridor (5643) J. Robertson, The Transport Treasury.

60058. BLAIR ATHOL returned to the south from time to time, as in late 1958 for instance, with a new double chimney on the Sunday 11.30 Kings Cross-Glasgow. It has been diverted via the New Line due to engineering works at Potters Bar and is climbing the Wood Green flyover. Boiler: 94A(27051) Tender: A4 Non-corridor (5643) Peter J. Coster.

60059. TRACERY on the 14.00 "Heart of Midlothian" from Platform 10 at King's Cross in August 1958. She had just been fitted with a double chimney during inspection at Doncaster, and despite having accumulated a good mileage, her driver thought she had just received a general overhaul! The 14.00 was only worked to Peterborough by the London engine, where a Heaton Pacific took over and the London engine returned on the up Glasgow-King's Cross express. The V2 arriving was No.60912 with a Leeds relief. Boiler: 94A(27075) Tender: GN (5284) Peter J. Coster.

60059. TRACERY pulls effortlessly out of Grantham past the Yard Box on April 5th 1961. Boiler: 94A(27075) Tender: GN (5284) Peter Groom.

60060. THE TETRARCH went north to Gateshead in 1939 and stayed there for 24 years overall, interspersed with spells as Darlington pilot and a sojourn across the Tyne at Heaton in 1962. No date or location is quoted but it looks fresh from Doncaster – otherwise it would dirty black – and its shopping dates were 8/51, 9/53 and 2/55 with the old totem and green livery according to Yeadon. The curious shed offices in the background, a pair of 1920s Art Deco semis complete with curved windows, reveal the location to be Darlington. Boiler: 94A(number uncertain) Tender: Non-corridor (5482) J. Robertson, The Transport Treasury.

60061. PRETTY POLLY at Leeds Central, 1 December 1954. The racehorse-owning LNER Board were doubtless blissfully unaware that the rest of us might find this a curious name for a locomotive. It gives a good view of the early BR ATC receiver and the protection plate – much narrower than the later and more familiar AWS arrangement. Boiler: 94A(27005) Tender: GN (5290) The Transport Treasury.

60061. PRETTY POLLY was indeed the unfortunate engine's name, and it was most unsuitable for an express locomotive, by a short head from one or two others. She was a hard working and regular performer however. On April 21st 1959 'Polly' is at Peterborough North with an up express. Boiler: 94A(27012) Tender: GN (5290) Frank Hornby.

60061. PRETTY POLLY was one of four A3s to have the small deflectors fitted in November 1959. They were in fact well nigh useless in strong wind conditions. She is seen approaching Cadwell, north of Hitchin, on the down slow with the 13.35 Kings Cross-Peterborough SO "parley" late in 1960. From here the down slow became the down goods, and unless intricate and little-used Block Regulations had been invoked, passenger trains had to be turned out, as can be seen from the position of the signals. Boiler: 94A(27012) Tender: GN (5290) Peter J. Coster.

60061. 'Polly' with wings sadly clipped, in charge of a long train of wagons in bitter conditions at Peterborough (that's the new goods depot in the background) in the dire winter of 1962-63. PRETTY POLLY went to Grantham in June 1963 and oblivion a few months after that. Boiler: 94A(27026) Tender: GN (5290) B. Richardson, The Transport Treasury.

60062. MINORU was for a short while the only A3 at Top Shed. She was a popular engine with the crews normally used to A4s. Late in the day for steam traction, Kylchap A3s took over the working of the "Yorkshire Pullman" whilst the A4s went farther afield. The high point of the evening rush hour was to see the down train and its immaculate A3, with double chimney and trough deflectors, striding effortlessly northwards. Here MINORU is north of New Southgate in September 1961 with the new Metro-Cammel Pullmans: there were no new Pullman brake coaches built, hence the retention of the older vehicles at each end. Boiler: 94A(27021) Tender: GN (5289) Peter J. Coster.

60062. A "Mensing Special". The photographer specialised in the pan shot, which involved taking the train broadside at a lower shutter speed while moving the camera with the engine, so that while the locomotive and train were sharp, the wheels and background were blurred, conveying a strong sense of speed. Not an easy proposition, but illustrations as sharp as this were his trademark. MINORU is approaching Peterborough on June 6th 1960 with what looks like the up "White Rose" or possibly a relief. The forward position of the double chimney on the smokebox crown is clearly shown; this was dictated by the presence of the superheater header behind the chimney casting. Although a great improvement in performance, it spoilt the side elevation of a very handsome locomotive. Boiler: 94A(27005) Tender: GN (5289) M. Mensing.

60063. Another long-term GN resident, ISINGLASS, in March 1961, heading the 9.50 Leeds-Kings Cross, having worked the "Yorkshire Pullman" the night before. Again the locomotive is magnificently clean. The A3 is coming up the long straight past Cadwell at a good pace. Boiler: 107(29295) Tender: GN (5231) Peter J. Coster.

60063. One of the most impressive angles of many engines is the passing shot, especially if one is alert or lucky enough to get the coupling rods near top dead centre. I was particularly pleased with this view of ISINGLASS in March 1961 since it shows what a superbly impressive and handsome locomotive Gresley's A3 was. It also emphasises the great size of the GN eight wheel tender. Boiler: 107(29295) Tender: GN (5231) Peter J. Coster.

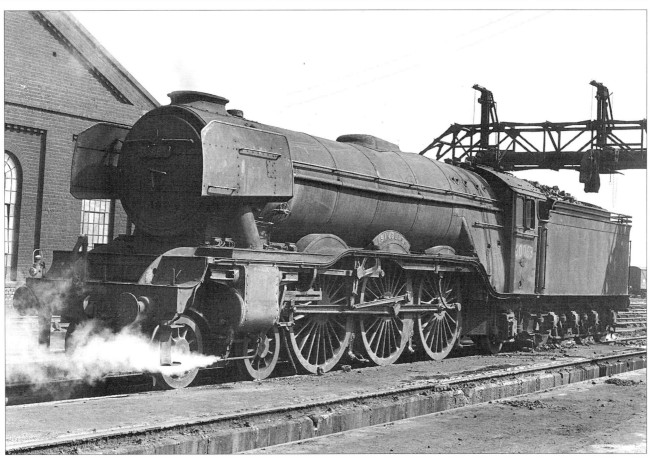

60063. ISINGLASS near the end, in what was, I am afraid, the external condition typical of New England's fleet for the many years that I knew it. It might be described as unlined grime! The lack of leaking steam suggests that her mechanical condition may be rather better, as the engines there often were. She is standing under the water gantry at New England shed – the date is not given but it would be 1962/63. Boiler: 107(29295) Tender: GN (5231) Barry Richardson, Transport Treasury.

60064. Scotland's first Pacific, allocated to Haymarket. She was first named WILLIAM WHITELAW after the Chairman of the LNER, but was rechristened in July 1941 when the name was transferred to A4 No.4462. No.2563 was obviously given prominence, and spent seven years on the summer non-stop "Flying Scotsman". She is seen here at Barkston triangle in June 1932, running in after a general overhaul at Doncaster Works. Boiler: 94 (7702) Tender: Corridor (5330) Cawston Bequest, Canon Brian C. Bailey collection.

60064. TAGALIE, as she has become, at Craigentinny sidings, near Edinburgh in 1947. Trains from the north that terminated at Waverley were often diagrammed to be worked ECS to Craigentinny carriage sidings by the incoming train locomotive. This saved two shunting operations in a busy station. Note the special bracket for the Flaman speed recorder. Boiler: 94A(9122) Tender: Non-corridor (5584) J. Robertson, The Transport Treasury.

60064. Now a Southern Area or Eastern Region engine, TAGALIE is at speed on the 14.10 Leeds and Hull relief. The photograph is at Hitchin, a surprisingly unusual shot for such a popular location. The driver standing by the down sidings adds to an excellent composition. There is no doubt that TAGALIE was moving fast! The date is April 12th, 1958. Boiler: 94A(27043) Tender: Non-corridor (5584) Frank Hornby.

60065. The second Pacific to be sent to Edinburgh, KNIGHT OF (THE) THISTLE remained a Scottish engine until July 1950, when four Scottish Pacifics were exchanged for four from Top Shed. Her name was altered in December 1932 and thus rendered incorrect both for the horse and the Order of Chivalry. The former Scottish KNIGHT OF THISTLE is at Grantham shed in her final condition, February 4th 1962. Boiler: 94HP(27062) Tender: GN (5285) J. Robertson, The Transport Treasury.

60065. KNIGHT OF THISTLE pulls away from Grantham with the first part of the up "Northumbrian", July 19th 1958. Boiler: 94A(27041) Tender: GN (5285) Peter Groom.

60065. KNIGHT OF THISTLE restarts the 13.21 "Parley" from Peterborough to Kings Cross from the up slow at Sandy. The slow train has doubtless been held here while up expresses clear the "bottleneck" through the station. The up expresses would have been going hard here, taking a run at the steady but lengthy climb to Stevenage. I wonder how many engines stood at this signal with an up freight, waiting for a margin! Boiler: 94A(27062) Tender: GN (5285) M. Mensing.

60066. MERRY HAMPTON, relatively new, stands at Inveresk with the 1.00 excursion to Newcastle on August 24th 1927. This early shot of the engine shows her virtually as built, with her original valves, boiler and tender, and the original North British works plate on the smokebox. Notice the Darlington reversing rod and the small bend at the base of the outside steampipes not yet hidden in the extended casing over the valve gear. Note also the connection to the pyrometer, an interesting but quite unreliable aid to the crew. Boiler: 94(7787) Tender: GN (5275) J. Rutherford, The Transport Treasury.

60066. The up "Yorkshire Pullman" was nearly always a Copley Hill duty, usually a Peppercorn A1. The crews worked to London and, after relief, worked the 15.45 "West Riding" back to Leeds, one of the longest turns of duty on the main line. On summer Saturdays, the timekeeping could be sufficiently poor for the up Pullman to be so late into King's Cross that the proper period of rest was not possible before returning north. Therefore the Copley Hill engine and men changed to work the earlier up Leeds express, and the King's Cross engine and men returning from Leeds worked the up Pullman. Here Top Shed's 60066 MERRY HAMPTON coasts at speed past a level crossing, which I think, is Helpston, in the summer of 1960. It is a good illustration of how much more difficult it was to get a pleasing composition with a good exhaust with Kylchap engines, especially in warm weather. Boiler: 107(29279) Tender: GN (5223) B. Richardson, The Transport Treasury.

60067. A poor old print, for which apologies must be due, but this is an unusual view of LADAS, then LNER No.2566, with a corridor tender transferred from No.2565, heading the northbound non-stop "Flying Scotsman" at King's Cross in 1929. Haymarket's fourth Pacific was less often used on this duty than the first two and 1929 was the only season in which she worked the duty. By the following year the A3s were brought into the operation and Haymarket's prolific Nos.2795 and 2796 tended to dominate. Boiler: 94(7788) Tender: Corridor (5330) Cawston Bequest, Canon Brian C. Bailey collection.

60067. LADAS many years later, then a London engine with a double chimney, starting the 14.00 from King's Cross Platform 6 in 1961. The locomotive would have worked the train as far as Peterborough where a Heaton Pacific would have relieved it. Boiler: 107(29277) Tender: Non-corridor (5479) Peter J. Coster.

60067. LADAS heads north with the 15.50 Kings Cross-Leeds express through the brand new down platforms at Hadley Wood station on May 15th 1959. No.69531 is on the down slow, a reminder of GN commuting in days gone by. On coming south, LADAS was allocated to the main GN sheds for a spell, although most of her time was as a Doncaster engine, where she was allocated at the time of the photograph. Boiler: 107(27016) Tender: Non-corridor (5479) John F. Aylard.

60068. The last of the first batch of Scottish Pacifics, the last to join the A3 class, and the most inaccessible to many, SIR VISTO stands at Hawick with a slow train to Carlisle. She was never allocated farther south of the Border than Carlisle, never used on the "Nonstop" and therefore never had a corridor tender attached. She was also an unusual sight south of Newcastle before the 1939-45 war, and an even rarer sight thereafter. SIR VISTO was the last Pacific to be fitted with a 220psi boiler and converted to Class A3 in December 1948, but by August 27th 1949 was work-stained and dirty. She still had right-hand drive and a 94HP boiler ordered under Thompson's stewardship. The burnt smokebox door was unusual, a sign of either a thrashing or failure to clear the smokebox properly on shed. Boiler: 94HP(8721) Tender: A4 Non-corridor (5637) J. Robertson, The Transport Treasury.

60068. A photograph both admired and envied by many. John Aylard was photographing by Wood Green Tunnel on March 11th 1961 when the 16.05 Dringhouses Class "C" freight from King's Cross Goods came through, hauled by no less than a pristine SIR VISTO, running in after general overhaul at Doncaster Works. One could count the number of sightings of this engine in London on one hand since the war. SIR VISTO, in common with the three other A3s at Carlisle Canal, never had AWS or trough deflectors fitted. She had been converted to left-hand drive, lost her A4 tender and had gained a 94A boiler. John F. Aylard.

60068. SIR VISTO at the west end of Haymarket shed on March 16th 1958. Boiler: 94A(27036) Tender: GN (5224) W. Hermiston, The Transport Treasury.

60068. SIR VISTO steadily accelerates the up "Waverley" away from Edinburgh through the Niddrie Junctions, a few miles outside the Scottish capital, on to the Waverley route. She will have to run steadily a few more miles clear of the colliery yards before taking a run at Falahill bank. The date is October 12th 1957. Boiler: 94A(27036) Tender: GN (5224) J. Robertson, The Transport Treasury.

60069. SCEPTRE was the first North Eastern Area A1 Pacific and one of the less frequent visitors down south after 1945. The A3 was allocated to Gateshead before the war, but to Heaton for most of the time afterwards. On April 28th 1956 she is easing an up express round the sharp curve at the south end of King Edward Bridge Junction before picking up speed. The train looks as if it is a cross-country express largely comprising LMSR stock. The tracks on the right went past Gateshead shed to both the High Level Bridge and the east end of Central station, or to Sunderland.. Boiler: 94A(27049) Tender: GN (5258) J. Robertson, The Transport Treasury.

60070. GLADIATEUR was reputed to be Gateshead's best A1 before the war. After rebuilding it continued as a NE engine, working from both Gateshead and standing pilot at Darlington. It is seen here in its final condition, waiting at King's Cross station engine yard for the signal to draw out and couple to her train. October 5th 1961. Boiler 94A(27069) Tender Non-corridor (5477) John F. Aylard.

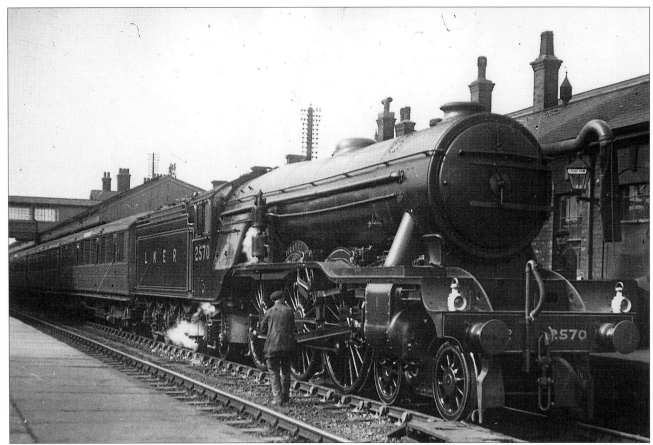

60071. TRANQUIL, as LNER A1 No.2570, pauses at Grantham with an up express. The driver is inspecting the motion for heating; note also the Westinghouse brake pump carried by the NE A1s. Grantham up platform south end was always a challenge to a photographer with its abundance of chimney stacks and protuberances to decorate the top of the boiler! The year is 1930. Boiler: 94(7798) Tender: GN (5280) Cawston Bequest, Canon Brian C. Bailey collection.

60071. TRANQUIL in final form, at Haymarket shed (an EE Type 4 lurks beyond). This A3 was a Gateshead engine for most of her life and Gateshead, and to a lesser extent Heaton, continued to share the work north with Haymarket both before and after the war. Tyneside Pacifics were usually present in numbers at Haymarket. The date is probably early 1962. Boiler: 107(29290) Tender: GN (5291, but changed to 5263 in 1963) J. Robertson, The Transport Treasury.

60072. SUNSTAR is unusual motive power for the 16.05 Kings Cross-Dringhouses freight, north of the old Potters Bar station and regaining the down slow after passing through the "bottleneck", August 1st 1952. SUNSTAR was a Gateshead stalwart before the war, but transferred to Heaton for most of her time post-war. She was one of the early rebuilds once it had been decided to reboiler the A1 class during the 1939-45 war, but she still retained right-hand drive. She was another A3 with a lower numberplate for a while, but she kept the same tender post-war, the prototype non-corridor high-sided version. Boiler: 94A(27079) Tender: Non-corridor (5476) John F. Aylard.

60072. A beautiful shot of SUNSTAR pulling away from Newcastle Central with a down express, April 14th 1957. Although Heaton always tended to keep their Pacifics much cleaner than their neighbours in Gateshead, SUNSTAR has not long emerged from overhaul at Doncaster. This is a particularly good illustration of a numberplate bearing the rogue "curly 6" in the Doncaster pattern maker's set. This figure was more rounded than the true Medium Gill Sans "6", which can be seen on the cab side. Boiler: 94A(27009) Tender: Non-corridor (5476) J. Robertson, The Transport Treasury.

60072. SUNSTAR at Haymarket shed two months later on June 16th 1957. Haymarket's COLORADO is in the background, and the named V2 is THE GREEN HOWARDS, a stranger from York. Boiler: 94A(27009) Tender: Non-corridor (5476) J. Robertson, The Transport Treasury.

60073. An up fast freight at Penmanshiel hauled by ST. GATIEN, May 21st 1956. The train is short but the containers suggests that this is perishable traffic – meat from the East Coast of Scotland, most likely. Fast freights were always part of the work of the Pacifics. Boiler: 94A(27030) Tender: GN (5278) J. Robertson, The Transport Treasury.

60074. HARVESTER, one of more renowned A3s, standing at York on a down express, August 16th 1952. Originally a Gateshead engine, it was involved in the skirmishing with Haymarket prior to non-stop running in 1928, and was fitted with a corridor tender. While at Haymarket it was used, among other things, to check clearances north of Edinburgh. Later it went to Neville Hill at Leeds, and worked between Leeds, York and Newcastle. Boiler: 94A(27010) Tender: GN (5268) J. Robertson, The Transport Treasury.

60074. HARVESTER, now with a double chimney, rests at Neville Hill shed, Leeds. The date is not given but it must be later than March 1959 since it has a double chimney. The contrast in appearance with the adjacent Ivatt 2-6-0 is striking. Boiler: 94A(27041) Tender: GN (5271) B. Richardson, The Transport Treasury.

60075. ST. FRUSQUIN, the solitary A3 without deflectors by then, standing as the pilot at Darlington shed on July 9th 1963. The Darlington reversing rod has survived, and there is a hint that the North British main steampipe covers have, too. The Smith-Stone speedometer fitting is clear in this view. A Gateshead engine for many years. Boiler: 107(29324) Tender: GN (5287) The Transport Treasury.

60076. GALOPIN, at an unspecified location and date. The type 94HP boiler pins us down to 1952-54 and the freshly repainted Q6 alongside suggests Darlington. As the locomotive shuttled between Gateshead and pilot duties at Darlington in the post-war years, Darlington seems most likely. Boiler: 94HP(27071) Tender: GN (5232) J. Robertson, The Transport Treasury.

60077. THE WHITE KNIGHT at Holbeck in May 1961. Formerly a Tyneside engine, following the administrative changes of 1957 she went to Holbeck in 1960. The loco had been cleaned especially as O.S. Nock was footplating later over the Settle-Carlisle route. Boiler 94HP(27046) Tender Non-corridor (5581) Peter J. Coster.

60077. LNER No.2576 THE WHITE KNIGHT at Grantham, fitted with the experimental ACFI feedwater heater and pump working with the 180psi boiler. The pump is clearly shown and there is no doubt that it ruined a handsome locomotive. The period is June 1930 and the engine has just been overhauled. Boiler: 94(7795) Tender: GN (5286) Cawston Bequest, Canon Brian C. Bailey collection.

60078. NIGHT HAWK at Haymarket on September 18th 1960 in the company of a named V2, which looks like THE SNAPPER from its nameplate and, unusually for Haymarket, a K3. Another long term Gateshead locomotive. Boiler: 94HP(27070) Tender: GN (5275) J. Robertson, The Transport Treasury.

60078. NIGHT HAWK at Darlington with a southbound cross country train. The date is July 31st 1958. Boiler: 94HP(27017) Tender: GN (5275) M. Mensing.

60079. LNER No.2578 BAYARDO at Grantham in the 1930-32 period. BAYARDO was the first Heaton A1 in October 1924, and was fitted with a 220psi boiler in 1928. Boiler: 94HP(8031) Tender: GN (5288) Cawston Bequest, Canon Brian C. Bailey collection.

60079. BAYARDO at Haymarket, with A4 GOLDEN PLOVER alongside, May 3rd 1959. The A3 had since been exchanged with CAPTAIN CUTTLE at Carlisle Canal in order that the new experimental livery should be more widely seen. No.60079 had just returned from Doncaster Works after a casual repair, during which the double chimney was fitted. Date Boiler: 94HP(27000) Tender: GN (5277) J. Robertson, The Transport Treasury.

60079. BAYARDO heads an up express past Ayton signalbox, some ten miles north of Berwick, June 3rd 1950. The box is not one of the S&T Dept's greater glories! The A3 is only a fortnight out of Doncaster Works after overhaul but that has not prevented a patina of grime settling on the clean paintwork. Nor, I suspect has the "Carlisle" on the buffer beam deterred one of the Newcastle sheds from giving the engine a little more running-in before reaching her home depot! Boiler: 94HP(27066) Tender: GN (5277) J. Robertson, The Transport Treasury.

60079 BAYARDO restarts a down express from Hawick. The engine is in a grubby state and is no doubt run-down and shortly due for overhaul. The Carlisle A3s shared the express and semi fast work over the Waverley route with Haymarket, but since there was not enough work to occupy all four when available, they worked to Newcastle and on parcels and fast freight on occasions. They were not kept particularly clean, as the photograph shows. A local resident, an ex-NBR 4-4-2T, is in the shed yard. Date - July 14th, 1956. Boiler: 94A (27050) Tender: GN (5277). J Robertson, The Transport Treasury.

60080. The up "Thames-Clyde Express" leaving Kilmarnock behind DICK TURPIN on June 22nd 1960. After many years at Heaton, No.60080 was moved to the former LMS shed at Holbeck to join a number of ex-Tyneside A3s, where they displaced the "Royal Scot" 4-6-0s from such duties as this. This engine was an oddity in that the rider rather than the horse is celebrated, contrary to LNER practice, and there is no trace of a winning racehorse carrying the name. Boiler: 94A(27065) Tender: GN (5229) Frank Hornby.

60081. SHOTOVER was the other Pacific fitted with an ACFI feedwater heater and pump, in this case working with 220psi. The location is unknown but Craigentinny seems likely. The date is not given but it must fall between 1929 and 1938. Boiler: 94HP (number unknown) Tender: GN (prob.5290) J.T. Rutherford, The Transport Treasury.

60081. SHOTOVER with 220psi boiler, corridor tender and Westinghouse pump – though the air brake was disabled. The Heaton engine is hauling the up "Flying Scotsman" and the date is certainly summer 1928 since that was the only year that No.2580 worked it. The train was probably non-stop, since later in the year the Haymarket A1s took over and in September, SHOTOVER returned to Newcastle. Boiler: 94HP(8029) Tender: Corridor (5326) Gresley Society Trust.

60082. NEIL GOW at Haymarket on June 21st 1959, in company with A4 WILLIAM WHITELAW, V1 No.67615 and an unidentified A3 – note the contrast in looks imparted by the single/double chimneys. Boiler: 94A(27015) Tender: GN (5226) J. Robertson, The Transport Treasury.

60083. SIR HUGO as LNER No.2582, probably standing at Craigentinny. The smokebox door burns mean this was not a late phenomenon! The date is something of a puzzle. The Westinghouse pump was removed in 1933 and the A3 became black in December 1941, so the date falls between those two years. The presence of the J39 might have helped in establishing the date, but instead we have a greater mystery, since only one bore the last three visible numbers '269', before renumbering (No.1269, later BR No.64731) and that was allocated to the GE Section. The Scottish Area had nineteen J39s by 1931, none of which bore those numbers. In June 1938, however, two J39s were loaned from the GE Section to Carlisle Canal, to work to Edinburgh, replacing K3s borrowed by the Southern Area, and although the engines were said to be Nos.1259 and 1942, it is always possible that No.1269 went as well or instead of. Boiler: 94(7696 or 7704) Tender: GN (5292 or 5282) W. Hermiston, The Transport Treasury.

60084. Post-war, TRIGO was one of the quintet at Leeds Neville Hill, used on the "Queen of Scots" Pullman and the "North Briton" service to Glasgow. She heads the up Pullman in this fine shot at Ousten, near Chester-le-Street, May 15th 1954. Boiler: 94HP(27073) Tender: A4 Non-corridor (5645) J. Robertson, The Transport Treasury.

60084. TRIGO, coaling at York shed in late 1947. The then Gateshead A3 had been overhauled with a new 94HP boiler and painted LNER apple green, but at the end of the year the livery had changed to reflect BR ownership. Boiler: 94HP(9567) Tender: A4 Non-corridor (5645)

60085. Heaton's MANNA, cleaned and painted in the short-lived BR blue livery, eases across the diamond crossing with the Scarborough line into York station. The date is not known but the BR blue livery gives us 1950-52. Boiler: 94A(27003) Tender: Non-corridor (5483) W. Hermiston, The Transport Treasury.

60086. The A3, kept well clean, was an enormously impressive and handsome locomotive especially photographed from a low viewpoint. This is evident in the case of GAINSBOROUGH, LNER No.2597, at the head of the southbound "Flying Scotsman" pulling away from Grantham in 1932. Boiler: 94HP(8225) Tender: Non-corridor (5478) Cawston Bequest, Canon Brian C. Bailey collection.

60086. GAINSBOROUGH, now with a double chimney, waits at the west end of Newcastle Central with an up Leeds express in 1960. Boiler: 94A(27052) Tender: Non-corridor (5478) Peter J. Coster.

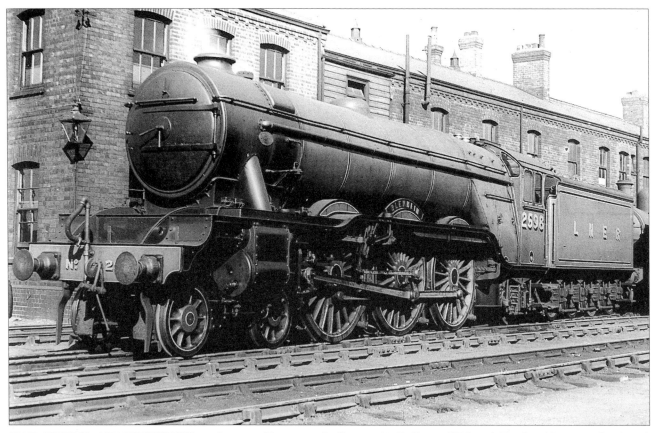

60087. LNER No.2598 BLENHEIM brand new at Doncaster in June 1930. Boiler: 94HP(8249) Tender: Non-corridor (5482) Cawston Bequest, Canon Brian C. Bailey collection.

60087. BLENHEIM was originally a North Eastern Area loco but after a time oscillating between Doncaster and Haymarket, she settled at the latter. Although one of the A3s called to deputise on the "Coronation", BLENHEIM became one of the rarest of visitors to the south end of the main line and also one of the least photographed. She is shown here at Haymarket in this splendid photograph, clean and resplendent in the apple green of the former LNER. I would imagine from her appearance that she has been recently overhauled and repainted. In the background is one of the J83 Waverley pilots. The period is 1948-50. Boiler: 94A(9449) Tender: Non-corridor (5572) W. Hermiston, The Transport Treasury.

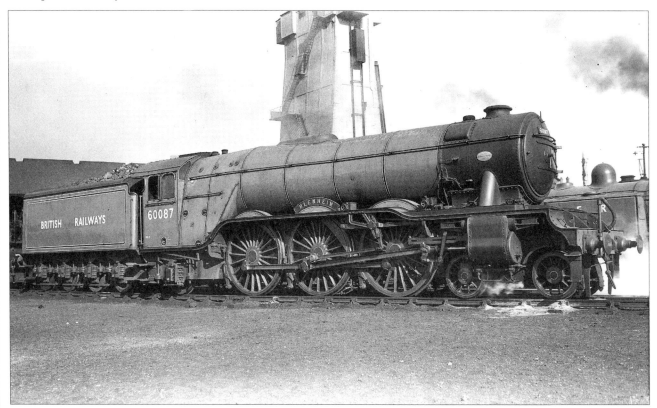

60087. BLENHEIM bursts out from the tunnel in Princes St Gardens, Edinburgh, with a down express for Aberdeen on September 3rd 1957. The first vehicle is a sleeping car, which is intriguing for an afternoon train; was it required at Aberdeen to strengthen an overnight express? Please note the A3 is, as usual for a Haymarket Pacific, very well cleaned. Boiler: 94A(27055) Tender: Non-corridor (5572) Peter Groom.

60088. BOOK LAW as LNER No.2599 at Grantham in summer 1930. It is probably brand new. Boiler: 94HP(8250) Tender: Non-corridor (5483) Cawston Bequest, Canon Brian C. Bailey collection.

60088. BOOK LAW at Haymarket in August 1959, a superb picture. It has recently been overhauled and fitted with a double chimney. This engine had oscillated between either side of the Tyne before it eventually became a long term Heaton favourite. Its condition contrasts strongly with the sister engine in the background! Boiler: 94A(27064) Tender: GN (5263) J. Robertson, The Transport Treasury.

60089. The first A3 to be built new, as distinct from rebuilt from an A1, was FELSTEAD. A Doncaster engine pre-war and the regular charge of Driver Watson, she moved south to King's Cross. She emigrated to Haymarket in 1951 and was there in company with sister engine PAPYRUS and a BR Class 5 4-6-0 on August 3rd 1958. Boiler: 94A(27072) Tender: GN (5255) J. Robertson, The Transport Treasury.

60090. GRAND PARADE. There were of course, two of them, as one was destroyed in the Castlecary accident in 1937. This is the original LNER No.2744, heading south out of Grantham with the up "Flying Scotsman" in 1932. In 1933 she was coupled to a corridor tender for the "Nonstop". Boiler: 94HP(8075) Tender: GN (5273) Cawston Bequest, Canon Brian C. Bailey collection.

60090. An interesting photograph indeed. GRAND PARADE stands at Newcastle Central at the head of the down "Coronation", no less. The problem with this locomotive is that the original and the replacement of April 1938 differ only in the boiler number and the tender number, neither of which are normally visible without very close inspection. Condition is no help as the A3s were usually well cleaned. Two dates are possible, one with the original and one with the replacement. The first is early July 1937, when the new train was worked from Doncaster to Edinburgh ready for the commencement on Monday July 5th. Willie Yeadon records that No.2744 was transferred from Kings Cross to Haymarket on July 7th and it would make sense to send her north with

the ECS. However, the locomotive is displaying "open lights", the express lamp code, and unless special authority had been obtained, normally reserved only for the empty Royal Train, it would certainly have been stopped by signalmen, since the bell description 2-2-1 would not tally with the headcode. The stock doesn't look pristine either. The more likely alternative is June 21st 1938, a day when the LNER management, uncharacteristically, took its eye off the ball. A4 No.4467 WILD SWAN was turned out for the "Coronation", but retired as early as Hitchin with a hot middle big end. The only replacement for Gateshead's Driver Walker to take north was a K3 No.2428 (BR No.61942). Quite unsuitable for the streamlined service, the K3 was replaced at Grantham by the second

GRAND PARADE, then only two months old, which worked through to Edinburgh, doing well in the circumstances to arrive only 38 minutes late. If this is the more likely, the fireman is taking no chances and watering the engine, and no doubt the Platform Inspector is anxiously willing the train on its way. Certainly the wheels, especially those of the bogie, suggest that the engine has not been out of Doncaster for many months. The replacement A3 was completed at Doncaster in April 1938 with the boiler off LEMBERG and the replacement tender was given the number 5263. She was sent to Doncaster shed since Haymarket regarded the new engine as "unlucky" and refused to accept her! 'MB' Collection.

60090. GRAND PARADE, now accepted as a Haymarket engine, roars up the last few yards to Penmanshiel tunnel with an up express on June 29th 1957, making a superb picture. The fireman has been working hard and no doubt is looking forward to a breather the other side of the tunnel. The former Southern Area engine was overhauled earlier in the year, but was clean and hard at work four months later. Boiler: 94A(27006) Tender: GN (5261) J. Robertson, The Transport Treasury.

60091. CAPTAIN CUTTLE, in BR green livery, pulls out of York near Holgate bridge with a southbound express past a popular photographic location, August 6th 1953. Until the advent of Mk.II coaches in the 1960s, coaches were carried on leaf springs which, in old age, had a somewhat uncertain geometry, as a glance at No.60091's train shows. CAPTAIN CUTTLE was a Heaton engine by then, and the Pacifics allocated there were kept a great deal cleaner than others were, notably those were from the other bank of the Tyne. Boiler: 94HP(27084) Tender: Non-corridor (5480) J. Robertson, The Transport Treasury.

60092. No. 2746 FAIRWAY on test with Sinuflo superheater elements in spring 1936. The train is the 11.04 from Doncaster, and the location looks like south of Peterborough. The King's Cross A3 still has the corridor tender it got from SHOTOVER in 1929 and the first vehicle in the very long train is of course the dynamometer car, now in the NRM at York. Boiler: 94HP(8028) Tender: Corridor (5326) C.C.B. Herbert, Gresley Society Trust.

60092. LNER No.2746 FAIRWAY at Greenwood with a lengthy up express, July 31st 1935. Boiler: 94HP(8028) Tender: Corridor (5326) H.C. Doyle, Gresley Society Trust.

No.60092 FAIRWAY stands at Newcastle Central ready to depart with an up express. The engine looks as though the date is in the early 1950s before AWS was fitted and, if I were to guess at the identity of the train, the 7.50 Newcastle - King's Cross, a Heaton turn as far as Peterborough. Alternatively, there were two other trains to Liverpool worked by Heaton. Tracks in stations such as Newcastle got little attention until something went awry, as the alignment of the tender and leading coach confirm. Boiler: 94A (probably 27003, 11 or 42) Tender: Non-corridor (5574).

60093. CORONACH stands outside Haymarket, ready to run to Waverley and pick up her train, May 26th 1957. The A3 is just back from general overhaul at Doncaster Works. Behind her are two A4s, KINGFISHER, the McLeods' regular engine, on the left and Jimmy Paterson's 60009 UNION OF SOUTH AFRICA on the right. Boiler: 94A(27031) Tender: GN (5287) W. Hermiston, The Transport Treasury.

60093. It feels like Haymarket on a Sunday morning early in spring. CORONACH stands at the west end, dead, maybe awaiting repair, maybe simply out of steam over the weekend. The tender shows surprising signs of an attempt at cleaning, a novelty for a Canal engine! The date is March 15th 1959. Boiler: 94A(27074) Tender: GN (5287) W. Hermiston, The Transport Treasury.

60093. CORONACH at Canal shed on September 18th 1961. The different firebox inspection holes of the Diagram 107 boiler from the 94 are quite obvious in this view. It is sad to think that six months later the locomotive was scrapped. Boiler: 107(29322) Tender GN: (5287) J. Robertson, The Transport Treasury.

60094. COLORADO ambling up the steep climb from Grantshouse to Penmanshiel tunnel with a fast freight. In the summer of 1948 this section was badly damaged by a storm and the resultant flooding, particularly of the unfortunately named Eye Water. The replacement underbridges, as pointed out in a similar view earlier, were of a LMSR standard reinforced concrete design with a distinctive parapet of concrete bars. A large span is by the first wagon of 60094's train, June 20th 1953. Boiler: 94A(27076) Tender: GN (5279) J. Robertson, The Transport Treasury.

60094. A splendid action shot of COLORADO hauling the up "Heart of Midlothian", a heavy train, nearing the top of the 1 in 96 of Cockburnspath Bank, May 21st 1956. The engine's exhaust has been lost against the bright sky. The ranks of trees, mainly conifers, were a nostalgic sight in those years, slightly reminiscent of the Canadian landscape, as the train pounded up the hill with the cutting and the tunnel a short distance ahead. When the "Heart of Midlothian" was introduced in 1951, it was entirely formed of BR Mk1 coaching stock, and I believe instructions were given to ensure that it remained so. Boiler: 94A(27013) Tender: GN (5279) J. Robertson, The Transport Treasury.

60095. As LNER No.2749, FLAMINGO pulls hard uphill on Borthwick Bank on the Waverley route with the up "Thames-Forth" express. From the look of the exhaust, her fireman is working hard as well! Borthwick Bank was also known as Falahill Bank, and was the hardest climb for up trains, lacking the opportunity to charge the bank at speed. The time is summer 1938. FLAMINGO was sent to Carlisle Canal within a week or two of completion and stayed there until withdrawal in 1961. Boiler: 94HP(8247) Tender: GN (5224) Cawston Bequest, Canon Brian C. Bailey collection.

60095. As a Carlisle engine, FLAMINGO was a very rare visitor to the capital. I doubt whether the sum of her appearances in the south in 32 years made double figures. A chance photograph of her, running in from Doncaster Works, shows her hauling a down goods from Peterborough past Highdyke signalbox and sidings in August 1952. Boiler: 94A(27023) Tender: GN (5224) Kenneth Wightman, P.J. Coster Collection.

60095. FLAMINGO at Carlisle Canal. Boiler: 94A(29299) Tender: A4 Non corridor (5637) October 21st 1959. The Transport Treasury.

60096. The fastest non-streamlined locomotive in the UK was camera shy in later years. Perhaps that had something to do with austerity and the availability of good film. It is a pity her achievement in 1935 was not commemorated, yet PAPYRUS was a favourite at King's Cross before the war and much photographed. There was even a rather fanciful book written about her. After the war she went to Haymarket and relative anonymity. Here she is standing at Waverley on February 24th 1952, beautifully cleaned and cared for. The front numberplate with its odd sixes and nines would have greatly offended the calligraphists among us! Boiler: 94A(27023) Tender: Non corridor (5581) J. Robertson, The Transport Treasury.

60096. PAPYRUS on the Eastfield turntable on June 3rd 1951, still in BR blue livery. Boiler: 94A (27023) Tender: Non-corridor (5581) W.G. Boyden, Frank Hornby Collection.

60096. PAPYRUS calls at Berwick with the up "North Briton", July 2nd 1955. Berwick was strange in that the down line wound sharply round the curved island platform and was restricted to 40 mph, while the up line was fairly straight through the station and was limited to 60 mph. It was not a good idea to confuse the two! Boiler: 94A (27065) Tender: GN (5270) J. Robertson, Transport Treasury.

60097. No.2751 HUMORIST departing from Grantham northwards in 1933-34. The Doncaster engine has had its smokebox modified with a sloping plate within the wrapper, under and in front of the chimney, together with a double chimney. The exhaust steam was directed through the leading chimney whilst the latter was used in an attempt to lift the exhaust with an updraught. The chimney was the ancestor of those used on the Pacifics post-war. Boiler: 94HP(8077) Tender: GN (5265) Cawston Bequest, Canon Brian C. Bailey collection.

60097. HUMORIST leaving King's Cross with the "Scarborough Flier" in August 1934. The Doncaster engine has another smokebox permutation, one which was used with the Mikados (albeit with a double chimney) and the initial design for the A4s. No.2751 has a single stovepipe chimney mounted on a sloping smokebox top, and small smoke deflectors. Boiler: 94HP(8077) Tender: GN (5265) C.C.B. Herbert, Gresley Society Collection.

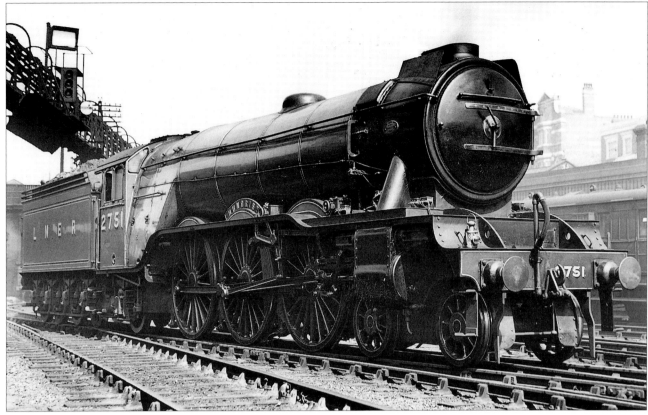

60097. A well-known view of HUMORIST, backing out of King's Cross. Now with a double blastpipe and chimney, the much experimented-with smokebox has been restored in full and decorated with small chimneyside deflectors in an effort to cope with drifting exhaust. The period must be 1938-39. Boiler: 94HP(8077) Tender: GN (5265) P. Ransome-Wallis.

60097. Retaining a sense of humour in her final form, HUMORIST at Haymarket on February 24th 1952, with sister A3 BROWN JACK and the rear of a Doncaster-built Peppercorn A1. By now she was fitted with smoke deflectors of the pattern used on the Peppercorn A1s. While they were more effective, they do nothing for the appearance of the locomotive. Boiler 94A(27041) Tender GN (5265) J. Robertson, The Transport Treasury.

60098. SPION KOP was a Doncaster engine for many years from new, although that didn't prevent being coupled to a corridor tender, briefly. She was never called upon to work the "Nonstop". Here she is working the up "Yorkshire Pullman", climbing from Grantham to Stoke – the date is given as 1932. The first two Pullmans form the portion from Hull. The engine is in surprisingly scruffy condition for the time. Boiler: 94HP(8076) Tender: GN (5226) Cawston Bequest, Canon Brian C. Bailey collection.

60098. SPION KOP, now a Haymarket engine, at her home shed. The date is not given but with the first BR tender emblem the early 1950s seem most likely. Boiler: 94A(27082) Tender: Non-corridor (5481) J. Robertson, The Transport Treasury.

60099. Haymarket's first two A3s became regulars on the nonstop "Flying Scotsman" and were deservedly famous. CALL BOY was the first, seen here with a rake of BR1 stock on the St.Pancras-Edinburgh express later to become the "Thames-Forth" approaching St.Boswells in August 1954. No.60099 was another of the A3s to be fitted with a smokebox door with the handrail mounted higher than usual and the numberplate beneath. Boiler: 107(29317) Tender: Non-corridor (5568) Cawston Bequest, Canon Brian C. Bailey collection.

60099. CALL BOY at Perth leaving with the 12.05 to Edinburgh, September 3rd 1955. Boiler: 107(29317) Tender: Non-corridor (5568) J. Robertson, The Transport Treasury.

60099. CALL BOY at Haymarket in her final form with a double chimney and trough deflectors, and a normally positioned numberplate, August 1961. Boiler: 94A(27064) Tender: Non-corridor (5568) J. Robertson, The Transport Treasury.

60100. SPEARMINT, the other famous Haymarket A3, at home in LNER apple green. She ran in this condition from early 1948 until late 1950, but the presence of the ferret and dartboard (visible on the original print, but not here) on the tender of the Director behind suggests that it would be later than her April 1949 general repair. Boiler: 94A(9117) Tender: GN (5283) J. Robertson, The Transport Treasury.

60100. SPEARMINT and her crew seem to be having a tussle drawing a train of empty coaching stock out of Leith Central station on June 13th 1953. There were many special trains in the Coronation year and it was likely that this was just such a service. Boiler: 94A(27036) Tender: Non-corridor (5566) The Transport Treasury.

60100. SPEARMINT at Eastfield with a double chimney in August 1962. The A3 now has the final arrangement of smokebox door with the lamp iron lowered, the numberplate on the top hinge strap, split handrail, trough deflectors and electrification flashes. Note when comparing with CORONACH that the LM and Scottish Regions applied the flashes in different ways. Boiler: 94A(27047) Tender: Non-corridor (5566) J. Robertson, The Transport Treasury.

60101. The third A3 was for some reason never used on the "Nonstop" and in fact became one of the most elusive of the class south of Newcastle. CICERO is at Haymarket on May 24th 1959 with V2 No.60965 and No.68481, one of the Waverley pilots. The V2 is from St.Margarets, but from its outward condition it appears to be on loan to Haymarket. Boiler: 94A(27083) Tender: Non-corridor (5571) J. Robertson, The Transport Treasury.

60101. CICERO backs down to Waverley past Princes Street Gardens on 25 June 1959; double chimney and AWS but no electrification flashes. CICERO never got the trough deflectors. Boiler: 94A(27083) Tender: Non-corridor (5571) J. Robertson, The Transport Treasury

60102. SIR FREDERICK BANBURY was the second of the two original Great Northern Pacifics of 1922 and, after 1945, became the only one. The first, No.4470 GREAT NORTHERN, by then of course had been transmuted, apart from its wheel centres, into an entirely new engine. In this view at Grantham, standing in the station on an up express, apart from the conversion to long valve travel, she is in original condition. The year is 1931. Boiler: 94(7772) Tender GN (5212) Cawston Bequest, Canon Brian C. Bailey collection.

60102. SIR FREDERICK BANBURY, the sole 'GNR' Pacific, at King's Cross with a SO relief to the "White Rose" in Platform 10, on a murky day late in 1957. The A3 had just returned to King's Cross from an eight-year spell on the GC Section. Peppercorn A1 No.60117 is alongside but neither seem to impress the guard, loaded with the trappings of office, making for the "White Rose". Boiler: 94HP(27000) Tender: GN (5292) John F. Aylard.

60103. An early shot of FLYING SCOTSMAN, still very much the GNR A1 with the taller chimney, cab and boiler mountings. She is hauling an up express and is leaving a very rural Wood Green Tunnel, past Tunnel box. The Pacific has a GN tender but still has the coat of arms on the cab side. She is equipped of course with right-hand drive, still with a square buffer beam, and still has short travel valves, all of which places the date between November 1925 and April 1927. Original Boiler: 94(7647) Tender: GN (5223) F.R. Hebron, Gresley Society Collection.

60103. FLYING SCOTSMAN at York depot on September 5th, 1954. The A3 has been converted to left hand drive but not yet fitted with AWS. Boiler: 94A (27074) Tender: A4 non-corridor (5640). Frank Hornby.

60103. FLYING SCOTSMAN heading the 9.20 from South Shields on August 18th, 1962 at Harringay West. The A3 is in her final condition and in five months time she had been handed over to Alan Pegler. In the background is the Harringay viaduct, its superstructure having recently been renewed. It was used to exchange traffic and locomotives between the up and down yards at Ferme Park yard without blocking the main lines. One can see a 350hp shunter on a transfer trip in the background. The down slow has been relaid with hardwood sleepers and the welded rail has been unloaded, ready for transposing. Boiler: 94A (27058) Tender: A4 non-corridor (5640). Alec Swain, The Transport Treasury.

60103. 4472 FLYING SCOTSMAN working an enthusiast special from King's Cross to York, May 1st 1966. The weather on this occasion was idyllic, and the old M&GN formation at Little Bytham the perfect vantage point to see the celebrated A3 climbing to Stoke at full regulator with the reverser well linked up. Boiler 94A(27048) Corridor tender (5325) Peter J. Coster.

60103. 4472 FLYING SCOTSMAN. A view of the famous A3 showing her corridor tender. She is at Marylebone as relief engine covering MALLARD and SIR NIGEL GRESLEY working an enthusiast specials to Stratford-on-Avon, October 12th 1986. Boiler 94A(27048) Corridor tender (5325) Revd Canon Brian C. Bailey.

60104. SOLARIO, one of the most celebrated of the A3s, when she was new, with ampersand L&NER on the tender. She also has taller boiler mountings, and I suspect is being turned at Hornsey, where there was a turntable long enough for the Pacifics when they were first introduced. The date is probably 1923-24. Original Boiler: 94(7694) Tender: GN (5224)

60104. SOLARIO, as LNER A1 No.4473 on the "Scarborough Flyer", which was worked by a Doncaster engine and men in both directions. She is approaching Finsbury Park from the north. The pre-war LNER scene is typical, with a marvellous signal gantry in the background. Mind you, in those days somebody had the stomach-loosening task of climbing up to replenish the oil in the signal lamps! The date is not given but is probably in the 1930s. Boiler 94 (Unknown), Tender GN (5254)

60104. SOLARIO, now LNER A3 No.104, but not for much longer, heads the up "Yorkshire Pullman" south of Marshmoor, near Hatfield, October 6th 1947. Boiler 94A (9483), Tender GN (5254) D.A. Dant, Gresley Society Trust.

60105. Those 'German' front ends could certainly look the part. VICTOR WILD and another (anonymous) A3 rest at the ends of Platforms 1 and 2 at King's Cross, in the period 1960-61. R.F. Orpwood, Gresley Society Trust.

60105. VICTOR WILD at the buffer stops of Platform (old) 7 at Kings Cross. The veteran of 1923 is standing next to a Brush Type 2 diesel electric of the then new order. This photograph shows clearly the arrangement of the trough type smoke deflectors at the front of an A3. It also shows clearly the extent to which snap head riveting has replaced the countersunk type. The period is 1960-61. Boiler: 94A(27070) Tender: GN (5225) B. Richardson, The Transport Treasury.

60106. FLYING FOX was a regular on the "Nonstop" from the London end. Overhauled and running-in, with corridor tender, she stands by the New England coaling plant on June 16th 1935. Boiler 94(7878) Corridor tender (5323) L. Hanson.

60106. Across the platform from No.60105 earlier, in the same period 1960-61, is another Grantham A3, FLYING FOX, in old Platform 8 at Kings Cross on another up express. Both Pacifics were almost forty years old with well over 4½ million miles to their credit. Boiler: 94HP(27063) Tender: GN (5212) B. Richardson, The Transport Treasury.

60107. Two superb shots of ROYAL LANCER, pulling away, north of Peterborough, with a southbound fast freight. No date is given but it must be 1962-63. Boiler: 94A(27044) Tender: GN (5267) B. Richardson, The Transport Treasury.

60107. Two views of an immaculate ROYAL LANCER with the 09.18 "White Rose" in March 1962. This was the only occasion, at least post-war, when a special headboard was carried by an A3. It was a special promotion by the Yorkshire Woollen Industry, and ran for a week or more. The first view is of the train leaving Kings Cross, and the second approaching Fletton Junction, south of Peterborough. Boiler: 94A(27044) Tender: GN (5267) John F. Aylard, B. Richardson, The Transport Treasury.

60107. ROYAL LANCER was another favourite on the "Nonstop", but that duty passed to the A4s and she received a GN tender once again. After the war she regained the LNER apple green livery and is in that glorious condition on May 17th 1948, heading the 13.10 Kings Cross-Leeds past Wood Green (Alexandra Park). This was the train used a month or so earlier for the Exchanges. Boiler: 94A(9515) Tender: GN (5267) Cawston Bequest, Canon Brian C. Bailey collection.

60108. GAY CRUSADER on an express in 1924-25. The date can be no later than her first overhaul in June 1925 since she is carrying the temporary number 1477N. The location is not clear, but the climb from Corby Glen to Stoke, just north of Corby Glen entering the cutting leading up to Stoke box (where there were indeed four tracks) is likely. The angle of the sun suggests that it was about midday. It might be an up train but there never was a down goods/slow between Stoke and Grantham South. Her train is a mouth-watering collection for the coaching enthusiast but I suspect the passengers thought otherwise! The bank has recently slipped by the look of the rock fill and counterfort drains. Original Boiler 94 (7698) and Tender GN (5228) M. Mensing/Osbourne Collection.

60109. Despite her name, HERMIT was no recluse, a grand runner and well liked for the main duties. Here she is backing out of King's Cross, bound for Top Shed on May 13th 1961. An engine in such condition would be unusual at the *start* of a journey in steam days, but HERMIT had just worked in from Leeds or Newcastle! Boiler: 107(27973) Tender: GN (5268) J. Robertson, The Transport Treasury.

60109. HERMIT at Peterborough with the down "Yorkshire Pullman", 13 June 1961. Boiler: 107(27973) Tender: GN (5268) 'MB' Collection.

60110. ROBERT THE DEVIL was thought by some to be named at the expense of Robert Thom, the Asst. Mechanical Engineer at Doncaster. Here she rests at King's Cross Top Shed with the first rebuilt Mikado alongside, April 30th 1958. Boiler: 94A(27025) Original tender GN (5230) J. Robertson, The Transport Treasury.

60110. ROBERT THE DEVIL about to start away from Grantham with an express for London in June 1958. It looks like a train from the Leeds area, since these were notorious for getting the brake ends anywhere but where they should be, i.e. at the outer ends of the train. Another picture showing good signalbox detail. How many times did we depart south from Grantham with the windows of the Yard box shaking as the engine lost her feet? Happy days. Boiler: 94A(27025) Original tender GN (5230) D. Beecroft, The Transport Treasury.

60110. ROBERT THE DEVIL at the summit of Stoke Bank, by Stoke box, with the up "Northumbrian" on August 26th 1959. The A3 is making light work of her 11-coach train, and the driver already has the engine well linked up for the sprint down the hill. Note the Gresley triplet dining car set. Boiler: 94A(27020) Original tender GN (5230) Peter Groom.

60111. ENTERPRISE as an A1 in late 1925, still much as she was built with taller boiler mountings, shorter valve travel, 180psi boiler, square buffer beam and right-hand drive, but renumbered at her first overhaul. She is on an up express between Great Ponton and Highdyke, just south of Great Ponton in the rock cutting. Again, her train is a coach enthusiast's delight. Original Boiler 94(7701) and tender GN (5231) M. Mensing/Osbourne Collection.

60111. ENTERPRISE, the first Pacific to classified A3, makes light work of the up "Yorkshire Pullman" south of Grantham. By this time she was LNER No.4480 and had a high-sided non-corridor tender No.5477, so the date is some time shortly after May 1938. Boiler 94HP(8082) Tender Non-corridor (5477) Cawston Bequest, Canon Brian C. Bailey collection.

60111. Over twenty years later, in the summer of 1960, ENTERPRISE races past Cadwell signalbox with a Newcastle-King's Cross express, apparently making light work of another quite heavy train. Boiler 94A(27025) Tender Non-corridor (5569) Peter J. Coster.

60112. ST. SIMON in early LNER numbering as 1481N, but with her buffer beam notched and the boiler mountings lowered. The date must therefore be later 1924/early 1925. The location is the same as that of GAY CRUSADER earlier, climbing to Stoke. Original Boiler 94(7702) and tender GN (5232) M. Mensing/Osbourne Collection)

60112. ST. SIMON, immaculately cleaned, with an express, probably from Leeds and Hull, south of the overbridge before Grantham in 1932. Boiler 94(7693) Tender GN (5232) Cawston Bequest, Canon Brian C. Bailey collection.

60112. ST. SIMON, still very clean but now as E112, draws into King's Cross with the up "Yorkshire Pullman", May 18th 1948. Boiler: 94A(8783) Tender GN (5211) Cawston Bequest, Canon Brian C. Bailey collection.

60112. ST. SIMON at Doncaster Shed – "Carr Loco" to Eastern men – just fresh from her last general overhaul in October 1962. One can see why a freshly painted A3 was such a glorious sight. Boiler: 107(29295) Tender GN (5289) W.G. Boyden, Frank Hornby Collection.

'60113'. 4470 GREAT NORTHERN in original condition with GNR numbering. She is on an express and seems to be going well. The location is quoted as Holme which means that it is probably a down train, since the down goods is evident, and the up goods was put in years later. The year is given as 1922. Original Boiler 94(7646) and tender GN (5211) Gresley Society.

'60113'. 4470 GREAT NORTHERN on a down express north of Potters Bar. The date must lay between 1928 and 1933 since the notching on the buffer beam is smaller than was later the case. Boiler: 94(7783 or 7765) Tender: GN (5227) Gresley Society.

Appendices

Appendix A.

BR No	NAME	Note	LNER No.	WORKS No.	BUILT	REBUILT A1 to A3	REBUILT Dbl. Chim	WDN	MILEAGE at 12/62
60035	WINDSOR LAD		2500	1790	10.7.34	A3	21.1.59	4.9.61	1,599,915
60036	COLOMBO	J	2501	1791	9.7.34	A3	14.11.58	23.11.64	1,524,372
60037	HYPERION		2502	1792	25.7.34	A3	8.10.58	12.12.63	1,685,060
60038	FIRDAUSSI		2503	1793	11.8.34	A3	30.9.59	18.11.63	1,629,619
60039	SANDWICH		2504	1794	9.9.34	A3	31.7.59	14.3.63	1,540,667
60040	CAMERONIAN		2505	1795	27.10.34	A3	16.10.59	6.7.64	1,510,657
60041	SALMON TROUT	E	2506	1797	19.12.34	A3	31.7.59	4.12.65	1,576,682
60042	SINGAPORE		2507	1798	1.12.34	A3	5.9.58	30.7.64	1,487,602
60043	BROWN JACK	D	2508	1800	9.2.35	A3	21.2.59	14.5.64	1,551,759
60044	MELTON		2543	1598	28.6.24	18.9.47	10.6.59	16.6.63	1,950,805
60045	LEMBERG	AJ	2544	1600	26.7.24	3.12.27	17.10.59	24.11.64	1,889,419
60046	DIAMOND JUBILEE		2545	1601	9.8.24	23.8.41	8.8.58	16.6.63	2,003,855
60047	DONOVAN	D	2546	1602	30.8.24	9.1.48	2.7.59	8.4.63	2,068,336
60048	DONCASTER	DI	2547	1603	30.8.24	16.5.46	29.5.59	8.9.63	1,879,139
60049	GALTEE MORE		2548	1604	27.9.24	13.10.45	4.3.59	29.12.62	2,000,566
60050	PERSIMMON		2549	1605	25.10.24	15.12.43	20.4.59	11.6.63	2,016,293
60051	BLINK BONNY		2550	1606	12.11.24	17.11.45	8.8.59	24.11.64	1,969,307
60052	PRINCE PALATINE		2551	1607	29.11.24	8.8.41	20.11.58	22.1.66	2,002,565
60053	SANSOVINO	D	2552	1608	11.12.24	2.9.43	12.11.58	27.5.63	1,944,665
60054	PRINCE OF WALES	M	2553	1609	31.12.24	28.7.43	29.8.58	28.6.64	1,811,007
60055	WOOLWINDER	I	2554	1610	31.12.24	3.6.42	17.6.58	4.9.61	2,022,833
60056	CENTENARY		2555	1611	7.2.25	16.8.44	15.7.59	13.5.63	1,867,962
60057	ORMONDE	E	2556	1612	18.2.25	11.1.47	19.9.58	28.10.63	2,132,842
60058	BLAIR ATHOL		2557	1613	28.2.25	8.12.45	3.10.58	19.6.63.	1,828,359
60059	TRACERY		2558	1614	25.3.25	25.7.42	17.7.58	17.12.62	2,515,318
60060	THE TETRARCH		2559	1615	28.3.25	16.1.42	14.3.59	23.9.63	1,966,363
60061	PRETTY POLLY	I	2560	1616	17.4.25	6.5.44	23.10.58	8.9.63	2,019,527
60062	MINORU		2561	1617	30.5.25	24.6.44	4.2.59	26.12.64	2,028,434
60063	ISINGLASS	C	2562	1618	27.6.25	6.4.46	6.2.59	28.6.64	1,894,169
60064	TAGALIE	DN	2563	23101	9.7.24	13.11.42	2.6.59	4.9.61	2,014,317
60065	KNIGHT OF THISTLE	DO	2564	23102	14.7.24	23.3.47	31.10.58	28.6.64	2,191,926
60066	MERRY HAMPTON	D	2565	23103	16.7.24	9.12.45	15.10.58	8.9.63	1,842,754
60067	LADAS	D	2566	23104	14.8.24	4.11.39	10.4.59	29.12.62	1,893,136
60068	SIR VISTO	K	2567	23105	14.8.24	10.12.48	9.4.59	1.9.62	1,746,759
60069	SCEPTRE		2568	23106	19.9.24	31.5.42	4.9.59	1.10.62	2,200,313
60070	GLADIATEUR	EL	2569	23107	24.9.24	18.1.47	25.4.59	4.5.64	1,900,000
60071	TRANQUIL	J	2570	23108	27.9.24	28.10.44	4.7.58	12.10.64	2,242,126
60072	SUNSTAR		2571	23109	30.9.24	12.7.41	24.7.59	22.10.62	2,241,966
60073	ST. GATIEN		2572	23110	3.10.24	10.11.45	15.8.58	19.8.63	2,347,825
60074	HARVESTER	BDJ	2573	23111	8.10.24	17.4.28	20.3.59	8.4.63	2,151,068
60075	ST.FRUSQUIN	J	2574	23112	11.10.24	26.6.42	14.8.59	13.1.64	2,158,777
60076	GALOPIN		2575	23113	14.10.24	27.6.41	30.6.59	29.10.62	2,141,355
60077	THE WHITE KNIGHT	F	2576	23114	19.10.24	10.7.43	1.4.59	13.7.64	2,138,058
60078	NIGHT HAWK		2577	23115	24.10.24	15.1.44	27.2.59	22.10.62	2,233,314
60079	BAYARDO	BK	2578	23116	29.10.24	22.5.28	18.4.59	16.9.61	1,944,756
60080	DICK TURPIN		2579	23117	3.11.24	26.11.42	13.10.59	12.10.64	2,114,947
60081	SHOTOVER	BDF	2580	23118	9.11.24	16.2.28	31.10.58	1.10.62	1,962,534
60082	NEIL GOW		2581	23119	30.11.24	15.1.43	18.9.59	2.9.63	2,169,980
60083	SIR HUGO		2582	23120	6.12.24	17.12.41	2.9.59	18.5.64	2,075,452
60084	TRIGO	J	2595	1731	22.2.30	A3	10.7.58	23.11.64	1,915,805

Continued

BR No	NAME	Note	LNER No.	WORKS No.	BUILT	REBUILT A1 to A3	REBUILT Dbl. Chim	WDN	MILEAGE at 12/62
60085	MANNA		2596	1733	22.2.30	A3	5.11.58	12.10.64	1,787,756
60086	GAINSBOROUGH		2597	1736	7.4.30	A3	12.6.59	18.11.63	1,783,937
60087	BLENHEIM		2598	1743	14.6.30	A3	12.8.58	28.10.63	1,954,902
60088	BOOK LAW		2599	1744	12.7.30	A3	1.7.59	14.10.63	1,945,415
60089	FELSTEAD	E	2743	1693	22.8.28	A3	9.10.59	14.10.63	1,845,593
60090	GRAND PARADE	D	2744	1694	23.8.28	A3	8.8.58	28.10.63	1,916,201
60091	CAPTAIN CUTTLE	E	2745	1695	8.9.28	A3	14.3.59	12.10.64	1,538,778
60092	FAIRWAY	D	2746	1700	26.10.28	A3	13.11.59	12.10.64	1,834,570
60093	CORONACH	GK	2747	1703	24.11.28	A3	19.12.58	28.4.62	1,645,866
60094	COLORADO		2748	1705	20.12.28	A3	26.8.59	24.2.64	1,677,014
60095	FLAMINGO	EK	2749	1707	26.1.29	A3	6.2.59	15.4.61	1,514,515
60096	PAPYRUS	D	2750	1708	23.2.29	A3	23.7.58	9.9.63	1,985,998
60097	HUMORIST	GH	2751	1709	7.3.29	A3	30.7.37	24.8.63	1,889,134
60098	SPION KOP	E	2752	1710	20.4.29	A3	17.7.59	28.10.63	1,695,383
60099	CALL BOY	D	2795	1738	19.4.30	A3	29.7.58	28.10.63	2,041,983
60100	SPEARMINT	D	2796	1741	17.5.30	A3	25.9.58	19.6.65	1,927,116
60101	CICERO		2797	1742	4.6.30	A3	20.2.59	11.4.63	1,815,153
60102	SIR FREDERICK BANBURY		4471	1539	10.7.22	16.10.42	21.4.59	11.11.61	1,905,170
60103	FLYING SCOTSMAN	D	4472	1564	24.2.23	4.1.47	24.1.59	15.1.63	2,065,842
60104	SOLARIO		4473	1565	17.3.23	11.10.41	24.4.59	7.12.59	1,874,150
60105	VICTOR WILD	D	4474	1566	24.3.23	1.10.42	6.3.59	16.6.63	2,214,515
60106	FLYING FOX	D	4475	1567	28.4.23	15.3.47	21.11.58	26.12.64	2,594,085
60107	ROYAL LANCER	D	4476	1568	26.5.23	4.10.46	2.6.59	1.9.63	2,156,626
60108	GAY CRUSADER		4477	1569	16.6.23	30.1.43	21.5.59	19.10.63	2,045,677
60109	HERMIT		4478	1570	30.6.23	16.11.43	12.3.59	29.12.62	2,069,511
60110	ROBERT THE DEVIL		4479	1571	25.7.23	8.8.42	30.5.59	23.5.63	2,118,692
60111	ENTERPRISE	B	4480	1572	17.8.23	15.7.27	5.6.59	29.12.62	1,937,026
60112	ST.SIMON	I	4481	1573	8.9.23	30.8.46	2.7.58	26.12.64	1,905,610
60113	GREAT NORTHERN	P	4470	1536	11.4.22	1.5.45		19.11.62	2,078,700

APPENDIX A: PRINCIPAL HISTORICAL DATA AND DIMENSIONS, A1 AND A3 PACIFICS

NOTES:

A	Fitted with 220psi boiler and cylinders lined to 18¼ins dia, 12/27
B	Fitted with 220psi boiler between 7/27 & 5/28
C	Fitted with Type "E" superheater 1925-1930
D	Coupled to a corridor tender between 1928 & 1936 and used on the Nonstop
E	Coupled to a corridor tender between 1928 & 1936 and NOT used on the Nonstop
F	Fitted with ACFI feedwater heater and pump, 1929-1938.
G	Modified experimentally to improve smoke deflection in 1933
H	Fitted with Kylchap double blast in 7/37
I	Fitted with small deflectors between 10 & 12/59
J	Carried experimental purple livery 1948-1949.
K	Never fitted with AWS or smoke deflectors
L	Estimated mileage at 1,900,000: 1,534,334 was recorded at 12/62
M	The original name was MANNA until 12/26
N	The original name was WILLIAM WHITELAW until 7/41
O	The name was changed mistakenly from KNIGHT OF THE THISTLE in 12/32
P	Rebuilt in 1945 to Class A1, later A1/1

(The Works numbers are either the Doncaster Works series or North British Locomotive Co.)

Appendix B.

APPENDIX B: PRINCIPAL DIMENSIONS, A1 AND A3 PACIFICS								
	A1	A1	A3	A3	A3	A3	A3	A3
Introduced	1922	1925	1927	1927	1934	1954	1937&1958	1958
Boiler Diagram no.	94	94(E type)	94HP	94HP	94A	107	94A	107
Boiler Pressure	180psi	180psi	220psi	220psi	220psi	220psi	220psi	220psi
Grate Area	41.25sq.ft.	41.25sq.ft.	41.25sq.ft.	41.25sq.ft.	41.25sq.ft.	41.25sq.ft.	41.25sq.ft.	41.25sq.ft.
Max Outside Diameter	6ft5ins	6ft5ins	6ft5ins	6ft5ins	6ft5ins	6ft5ins	6ft5ins	6ft5ins
Min Outside Diameter	5ft9ins	5ft9ins	5ft9ins	5ft9ins	5ft9ins	5ft9ins	5ft9ins	5ft9ins
Tube length	19ft	19ft	18.98	18.98	18.98	17.98	18.98	17.98
No. tubes	168	45	125	125	125	121	125	121
No. superheater flues	32	124	43	43	43	43	43	43
Heating Surface Area:-								
Firebox	215	215	215	215	215	231	215	231
Tubes	1880	507	1399	1399	1399	1281	1399	1281
Flues	835	2159	1123	1123	1123	1064	1123	1064
Subtotal (Evaporative)	2930	2877	2737	2737	2737	2576	2737	2576
Superheater	525	1104	706	706	706	749	706	749
Total	3455	3981	3443	3443	3443	3325	3443	3325
Wheel Diameter:-								
Bogie	3ft 2ins	3ft 2ins	3ft 2ins	3ft 2ins	3ft 2ins	3ft 2ins	3ft 2ins	3ft 2ins
Coupled	6ft 8ins	6ft 8ins	6ft 8ins	6ft 8ins	6ft 8ins	6ft 8ins	6ft 8ins	6ft 8ins
Trailing	3ft 8ins	3ft 8ins	3ft 8ins	3ft 8ins	3ft 8ins	3ft 8ins	3ft 8ins	3ft 8ins
Cylinders (3)	20x26ins	20x26ins	20ins then 19x26ins	18.25x26ins	19x26ins	19x26ins	19x26ins	19x26ins
Piston Valve Diameter (all variations)	8 ins	8 ins	8 ins	8 ins	8 ins	8 ins	8 ins	8 ins
Single Blastpipe orifice (sq.ins)	23.60	23.60	23.60	23.60	23.60	23.60		
Double Blastpipe orifice (sq.ins)							39 approx	39 approx
Tractive Effort (lbs) at 85% BP	29835	29835	36465 then 32909	30362	32909	32909	32909	32909
Total length, with Corr tender	70.28 ft	N/A	70.28 ft	N/A	70.28 ft	N/A	70.28 ft	N/A
Total length, with NC tender	70.43 ft	70.43 ft	70.43 ft	70.43 ft	70.43 ft	70.43 ft	70.43 ft	70.43 ft
Locomotive Weight (tons)	92.45	N/A	96.25	N/A	96.25	N/A	96.25	N/A
Tender details								
Type	GN type	Corridor	Non-corr	A4 non corr				
Coal	8 tons	9 tons	8 tons	9 tons				
Water	5,000 galls	5,000 galls	5,000 galls	5,000 galls				
Weight	56.30	62.40	57.90	60.35				

Appendix C.

APPENDIX C: MILEAGE

Year	No.	Scottish Region Mileage	Avail%	No.	North Eastern Region Mileage	Avail%	No.	Eastern Region Mileage	Avail%	Totals & Averages Mileage	Ave Mlge	Avail%
1950	17	52,781	73	60	46,471	68				3,685,537	47,864	69
1951	19	58,474	78	59	49,806	71		Included		4,049,560	51,917	72
1952	19	53,912	72	59	45,378	70		in		3,701,630	47,457	70
1953	19	54,831	75	59	48,207	71		N.E.		3,886,002	49,821	72
1954	19	57,999	78	59	51,137	72		Region		4,119,064	52,809	73
1955	19	57,435	75	59	51,288	69				4,117,257	52,785	70
1956	19	61,248	79	59	51,173	70				4,182,919	53,627	72
1957	19	65,783	80							1,249,877	65,783	80
1958	15	65,412	75				29	54,621	70	2,565,189	58,300	72
1959	15	65,511		30	51,374		28	54,001		4,035,913	55,286	
1960	15	62,102		30	45,914		28	52,131		3,768,648	51,625	
1961	14	53,074		30	36,517					1,838,546	41,785	
Totals		708,562			477,265			160,753		41,200,142	51,629	72
Averages		59,047	57		47,727	70		53,584	70			
Loco-years	209	12,340,788		504	24,054,156		85					

Appendix D.

APPENDIX D: COMPARISON BETWEEN PRE-WAR AND POST-WAR UTILISATION

(Operating stock is given in loco-years, fractions being due to a locomotive being transferred to another Region and hence working less than a year)

	YEAR	Class A1/A10	Class A3	+ or - ,(%)
	1937			
Operating Stock		42.00	21.52	
(Loco-Years %)				
Total Class Mileage		3,049,578	1,678,947	
Av. Annual Mileage		72,609	78,018	
	1950			
Operating Stock		0	60	
(Loco-Years %)				
Total Class Mileage		0	2,788,260	
Av. Annual Mileage		0	46,471	-40.44
	1953			
Operating Stock		0	59	
(Loco-Years %)				
Total Class Mileage		0	2,844,213	
Av. Annual Mileage		0	48,207	-38.21

Appendix E.

NOVEMBER, 1929.   THE RAILWAY ENGINEER.

IMPROVED TYPE FEED WATER HEATING APPARATUS, L.N.E.R.

Particulars of the New A.C.F.I. Apparatus fitted to two of the Pacific type Locomotives.

An improved type of A.C.F.I. feed water heating apparatus has recently been fitted to Pacific type engines No. 2580 *Shotover* and No. 2576 *White Knight* on the London & North Eastern Railway. The standard type of A.C.F.I. heaters, consisting of two circular chambers located on top of the boiler behind the chimney, have been superseded by a heater arranged to fit into the

increased in the pipe above the pre-arranged height, the extra weight of oil and water lifts the valve, and allows the excess oil and water to run to waste.

A similar type of overflow valve " K " is fitted to the hot-water chamber to control the return of excess water to the suction vessel. A horizontal tandem pump, consisting of a steam cylinder driving direct two water

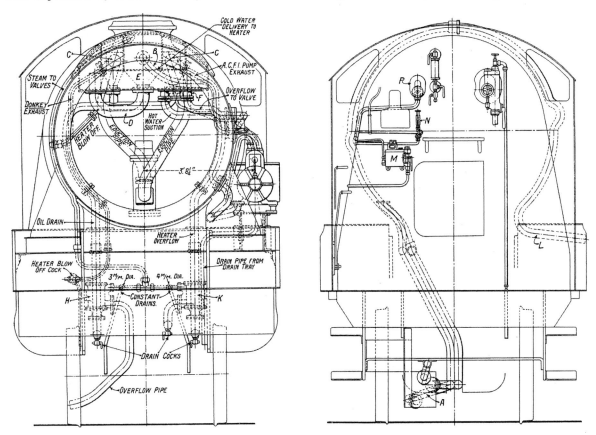

Cross Sections through Smokebox and Cab, showing details of A.C.F.I. Apparatus, Pacific Locomotive, L.N.E.R.

smokebox ahead of the chimney. This arrangement eliminates heat losses by radiation, and reference to the photographs reproduced will show that the appearance of the locomotive is not impaired.

The system employed is the " Integral Type," and differs from the " R.M." type previously used, in that the condensation of the exhaust steam by the cold feed water takes place at the pressure of the exhaust steam, instead of at atmospheric pressure, thus giving a correspondingly increased temperature of feed. No control valve is fitted on the exhaust steam pipe between the blast pipe and heater. Flooding of the heater is prevented by the oil drain and security valve " H." This is a piston type of valve proportioned to balance the weight of the valve, plus load on valve due to steam pressure in the heater, against a column of oil and water about one metre in height. If the height of this column is

cylinders, one hot water and one cold water, is fitted. The cold-water cylinder of the pump lifts cold water from the suction vessel " A," whence it has flowed by gravity from the tender, into the mixing chamber of heater " B." The cold water is introduced into the mixing chamber in the form of a fine rose spray, where it mingles with and condenses the exhaust steam from the blast pipe, that has passed through the oil separators " C, C'," thus absorbing the heat of the exhaust steam, and increasing the weight of water by the weight of steam condensed. The exhaust steam from the Westinghouse pump and the A.C.F.I. pump is also turned into the mixing chamber, thus increasing the efficiency of the apparatus.

The hot water then flows through the connection pipe " D " to the hot-water chamber " E," which it fills up to the height of the overflow pipe " F." By gravity the hot water flows to the hot-water cylinder of the pump,

THE RAILWAY ENGINEER.

which delivers it to the boiler through the check valve "G." The oil drain and security valve "H," before mentioned, evacuates the separated oil from the oil separators "C, C." This valve also ensures the safety of the apparatus from the danger of the heater flooding, owing to the incrustation of the return pipe or a valve sticking on the pump.

The pump is arranged to deliver a greater quantity of cold water to the heater than hot water to the boiler. It is to control this excess water plus the condensed steam that the return valve "K," is fitted. When water overflows into the level pipe "F," it flows to the underside of the valve, and when sufficient weight of water has collected it lifts the valve, and flows back to the suction vessel. On this return water pipe, an atmospheric pipe "L," is fitted. This atmospheric pipe, which is in the form of an inverted U tube, running over the boiler, prevents excess pressure being built up in the pipe system. In practice, there is thus a constant circulation throughout the apparatus.

A mechanical lubricator "M" is fitted on the backplate of the boiler in the cab, worked by impulse from the pump to ensure a constant supply of oil to

the pump, proportional to its speed. A manual lever is also fitted on the lubricator to flood the oil pipes at starting; this handle is also a useful indicator of the speed of working of the pump, as the handle lifts simultaneously with each stroke of the pump. A thermometer "N," on the cab indicates the temperature at which the feed water is delivered to the boiler.

The speed of the pump is controlled by a steam regulator cock "P," conveniently fitted in the cab. The apparatus is automatic in action; after the pump has been set to feed in proportion to the mean steam consumption of the locomotive no further attention is required. All pipe joints in the smokebox are of the lenticular self-adjusting type, and all hot-water pipes are asbestos lagged. The pump is carried on a beam, which forms a well for the waste water from the cylinder water cocks of the pump. The beam is secured to the motion bracket at the front end, and to the quadrant lever bracket at the rear end.

Engine No. 2580 is fitted with a high-pressure boiler working at 220 lb. per sq. in., while engine No. 2576 is pressed at 180 lb. per sq. in.

Arrangement of A.C.F.I. Feed Water Heating Apparatus in Smokebox, Pacific Locomotive.

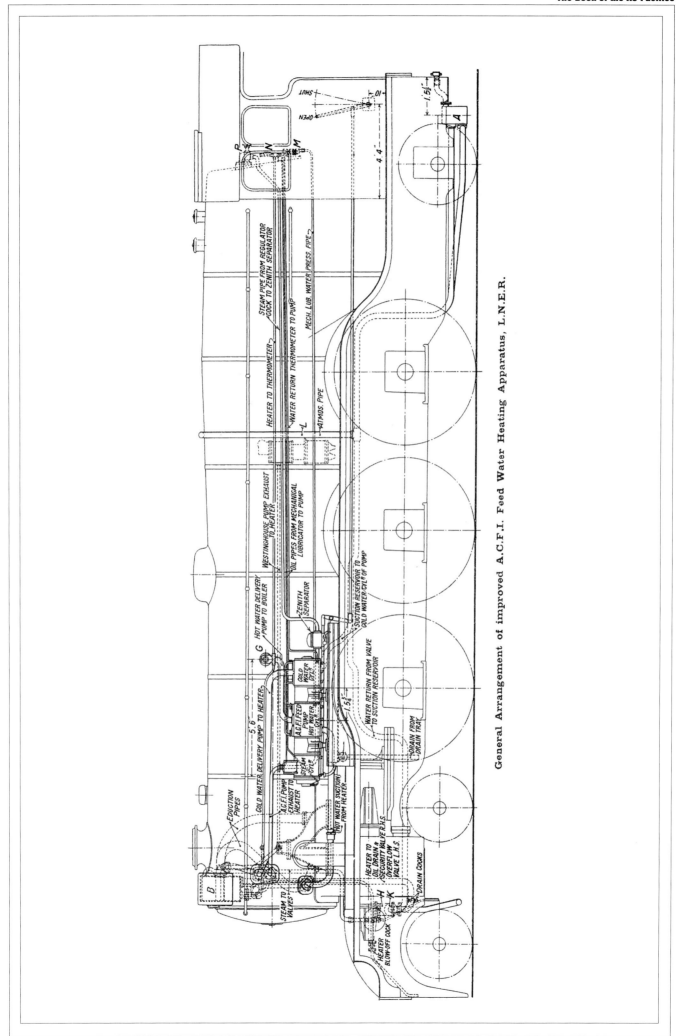

General Arrangement of improved A.C.F.I. Feed Water Heating Apparatus, L.N.E.R.

Appendix F.

LONDON & NORTH EASTERN RAILWAY.

MEMORANDUM TO THE   3rd June 1925.

LOCOMOTIVE COMMITTEE.

LOCOMOTIVE TRIALS.

G.W. ENGINE and L.N.E.R. ENGINE.

The trials extending over the week ending May 2nd between the Great Western Castle Class engine and the London and North Eastern Pacific engine, which have caused a great amount of public interest, have shown that each engine was able to undertake the work of the other, and maintain the time schedules with ease. On every run made by the Great Western Railway Engine on the L.N.E.R. system and the L.N.E.R. engine on the Great Western system, time was made up and in no case was time lost by the Engine.

The coal consumption of the engines when working over the Great Western system was as follows:-

        Great Western engine........42 lbs per mile.
        L.N.E.R.   " ....48 "   "   "
           Difference 6 lbs.
When working over the L.N.E.R. system -

        Great Western engine........53.4 lbs per mile.
        L.N.E.R.   " ....57.1 "   "   "
           Difference 3.7 lbs.

The characteristics of the two engines are dissimilar, as the following table shows:-

	Great Western Engine.	L.N.E. Engine.
Type	4-6-0	4-6-2
Cylinders	4	3
Tractive Power	31,625 lbs.	29,835 lbs.
Cylinder H.P.	2030	1946
Boiler H.P.	1440	1815
Boiler Pressure	225	180
Weight of Engine	79 tons 17 cwts.	92 tons 9 cwts.
Weight of Tender	40 tons	56 tons 6 cwts.
Total weight.	119 tons 17 cwts	148 tons 15 cwts.
Capacity of Tender - Coal	6 tons	8 tons
Water	3500 gallons	5000 gallons.

- 2 -

The narrow type firebox of the G.W. engine is more suitable for Welsh coal than the wide shallow firebox of the L.N.E. engine. When burning Yorkshire coal a thin fire is necessary; therefore the firebox of the L.N.E. engine should be the most suitable.   I anticipated that on Welsh coal the G.W. engine would probably be the more economical, but expected that with Yorkshire coal the L.N.E. engine would give the better results.

Conclusive results, however, cannot be obtained from such a short trial, and so far as burning Yorkshire coal is concerned, I am confident that if the trial had been extended, the position would have been reversed.

The average coal consumption of all Pacific engines over the whole of last year running on the L.N.E. system was 54 lbs per mile, the lowest on the G.N. section being 47 lbs per mile, the weight of the trains hauled running up to 550 tons.

The high boiler pressure of the G.W. engine tends to economy in coal, but involves higher cost in boiler maintenance. Although the tractive effort of the G.W. engine is higher than that of the L.N.E. engine, the boiler power is considerably less. Fast running was therefore made by the G.W. engine on short rising gradients, such as London to Finsbury Park, but on the long hill grades of the G.W. system, the Pacific engine ran faster.   As to high speed running on the flat and down grades, there is nothing to choose between the two engines, which are both very free running and capable of running at high speeds.

The trials show that the road bed of the L.N.E. is superior to that of the Great Western. The Pacific engine could not safely be run at such high speeds on falling grades on the Great Western road as their own engines, probably due to the greater length, weight and height of the Pacific engine. Strict observation had therefore to be observed on the speed limits

-3-

on the curves and crossings by the Pacific engine, and consequently higher speeds were required on the up grades to maintain the schedules. The higher coal consumption is partially consequent upon this.

It was arranged, before the trials were started, between Mr Collett the Chief Mechanical Engineer and myself, that no results should be published without our mutual concurrence; this agreement has not been kept. The Great Western Publicity Department have obtained all the data and furnished them to the Press for advertising purposes.

When it is remembered that the trials over the Great Western system consisted of only three trips - London to Plymouth and back - by the L.N.E. engine, it will be realised that no conclusive results could be arrived at.

Appendix G.

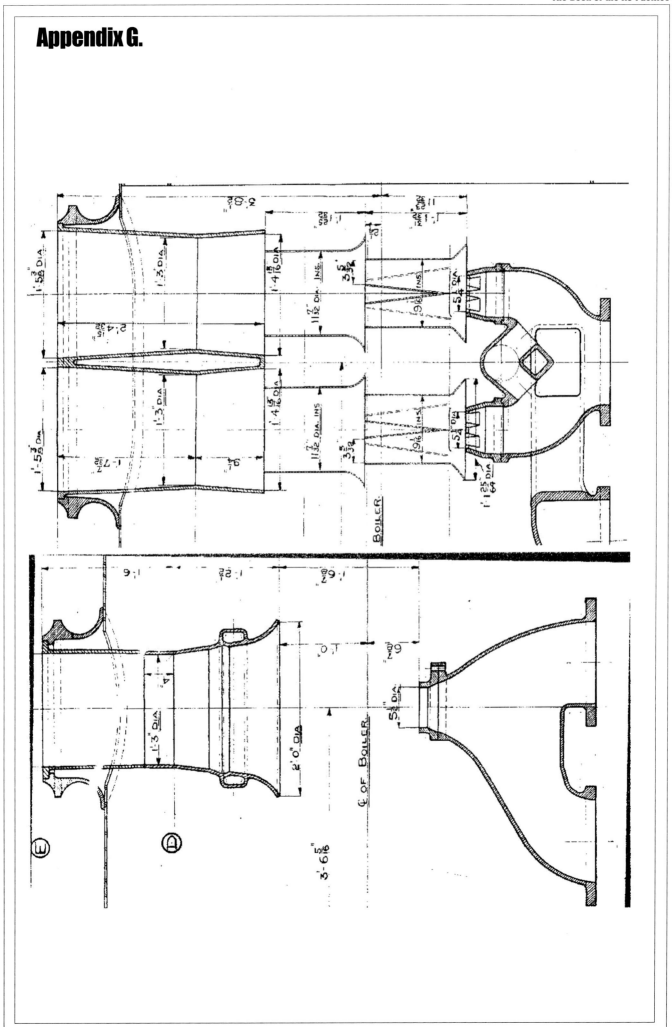

Appendix H.

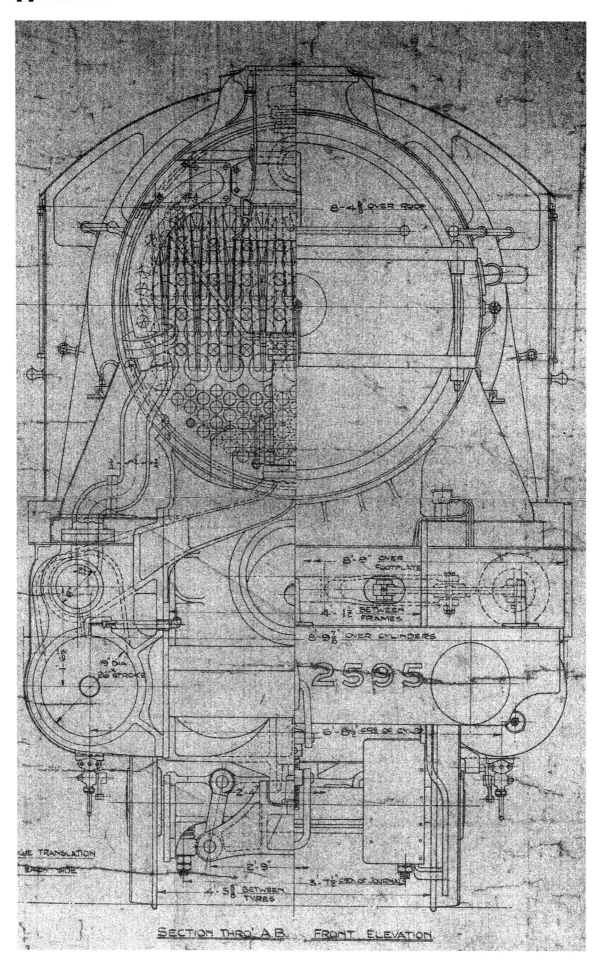

SECTION THRO' A.B.   FRONT ELEVATION

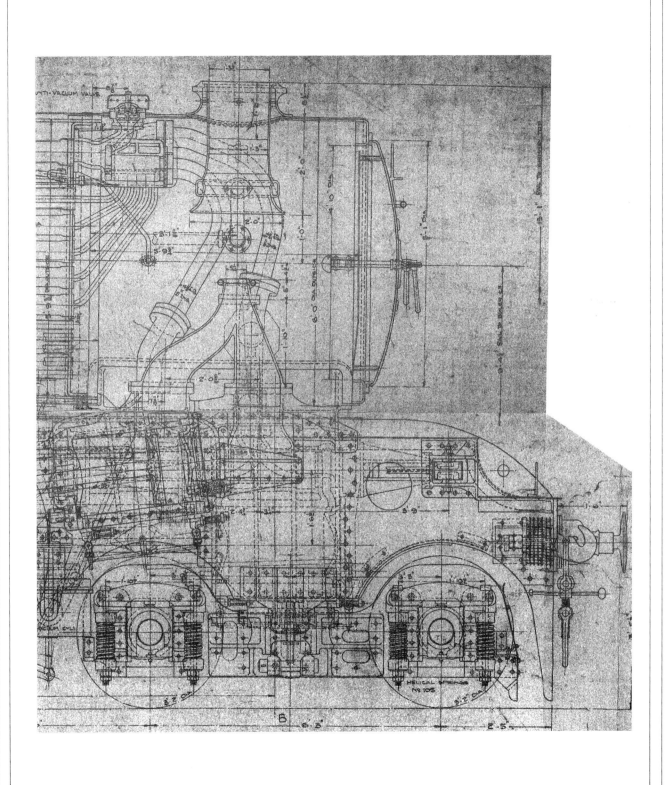

ENDPIECE